Complete
Wide Receiver

Jay Norvell

Human Kinetics

Library of Congress Cataloging-in-Publication Data

Norvell, Jay, 1963-
  Complete wide receiver / Jay Norvell.
    p. cm.
  1. Wide receivers (Football)--Training of. 2. Football--Offense. I. Title.
  GV951.25.N67 2012
  796.3322--dc23
                           2012021306

ISBN-10: 1-4504-2455-4 (print)
ISBN-13: 978-1-4504-2455-4 (print)

Acquisitions Editor: Justin Klug; **Developmental Editor:** Cynthia McEntire; **Assistant Editor:** Elizabeth Evans; **Copyeditor:** Patrick Connolly; **Permissions Manager:** Martha Gullo; **Graphic Designer:** Nancy Rasmus; **Graphic Artist:** Tara Welsch; **Cover Designer:** Keith Blomberg; **Photograph (cover):** John Sommers/Icon SMI; **Photographs (interior):** Neil Bernstein; **Visual Production Assistant:** Joyce Brumfield; **Photo Production Manager:** Jason Allen; **Art Manager:** Kelly Hendren; **Associate Art Manager:** Alan L. Wilborn; **Illustrations:** Tammy Page; **Printer:** United Graphics

Human Kinetics books are available at special discounts for bulk purchase. Special editions or book excerpts can also be created to specification. For details, contact the Special Sales Manager at Human Kinetics.

Printed in the United States of America   10   9   8   7   6   5   4   3   2   1

The paper in this book is certified under a sustainable forestry program.

Human Kinetics
Website: www.HumanKinetics.com

United States: Human Kinetics
P.O. Box 5076
Champaign, IL 61825-5076
800-747-4457
e-mail: humank@hkusa.com

Canada: Human Kinetics
475 Devonshire Road Unit 100
Windsor, ON N8Y 2L5
800-465-7301 (in Canada only)
e-mail: info@hkcanada.com

Europe: Human Kinetics
107 Bradford Road
Stanningley
Leeds LS28 6AT, United Kingdom
+44 (0) 113 255 5665
e-mail: hk@hkeurope.com

Australia: Human Kinetics
57A Price Avenue
Lower Mitcham, South Australia 5062
08 8372 0999
e-mail: info@hkaustralia.com

New Zealand: Human Kinetics
P.O. Box 80
Torrens Park, South Australia 5062
0800 222 062
e-mail: info@hknewzealand.com

E5675

Complete
Wide Receiver

CONTENTS

FOREWORD

During my four seasons as head coach of the Indianapolis Colts, from 1998 to 2001, I had the pleasure of working with Jay Norvell, who did a great job of coaching our wide receivers. I did not know Jay before we hired him, but he was very impressive in his interview and his recommendations were outstanding. We drafted Peyton Manning in 1998, and with the input of offensive coordinator Tom Moore, Jay Norvell, the other offensive coaches, and some good players, we were able to develop one of the most prolific passing attacks in the NFL.

Jay has extensive experience coaching wide receivers at both the college and NFL levels. At Indianapolis he coached future Hall-of-Famers Marvin Harrison and Reggie Wayne. Both were 6 feet tall but Harrison was slightly built weighing about 180 and very fast, running a 4.31 in the 40-yard dash. Wayne weighed 20 pounds more than Marvin and ran the 40 in 4.6. Although they were physically different in stature and speed, under the coaching of Jay and through a lot of hard work both have had fabulous careers and are headed to the Pro Football Hall of Fame.

Like the title of his book *Complete Wide Receiver*, Jay is the complete wide receiver coach. A lot goes into being a complete wide receiver, but to break it down into simple terms it involves three areas: getting open, catching the ball, and blocking for running plays. All three areas are discussed in detail in the book. Not only is Jay very knowledgeable about football, the passing game, and wide receiver play, he is also familiar with defensive strategy and how to attack it by throwing the football. As a coach, he is organized, has a terrific work ethic, and is very demanding of his players.

This book is more valuable today than a few years ago because the passing game has become more a part of offensive strategy then it used to be. The NFL is now a passing league, and you cannot win unless you have great success passing the football. In college games, you will see the quarterback more often in shotgun position than under center with three, four, and sometimes five receivers spread out from sideline to sideline. This puts stress on the defense, and the offense can be more effective passing the football. It also means more wide receivers are involved and their quality of play becomes more important.

In *Complete Wide Receiver*, Jay explains what it takes to be a great wide receiver and more important how to get there. Not only does he thoroughly cover the physical aspects of success but also the required intangibles. Among other things, he writes about work ethic, preparation, toughness, playing smart, concentration, and adjustments to different game situations.

This is the best and most complete book about wide receiver play that I have ever read. It is all you will ever need to play or coach the position and play or coach it the right way.

Jim Mora

ACKNOWLEDGMENTS

The influences that had a direct effect on the content of this book have also shaped my life as a coach, husband, father, and man. To all the coaches I played for all the way back to Jim Kotoski and the Meadowood Monsters in Madison, Wisconsin, to Frank Zuerner, Gary Kolpin, and Wally Schoessow at Memorial High School, to Hayden Fry at the University of Iowa, to Dan Reeves at the Denver Broncos, and Mike Ditka of the Chicago Bears. These men taught me how to play the game the right way.

To the head coaches I have worked for at the college and professional levels: Hayden Fry, Lou Holtz, Terry Allen, Barry Alvarez, Dan McCarney, Jim Mora Sr., Bill Callahan, Karl Dorrell, and Bob Stoops. Not only have these men become great mentors and examples to me, but they have also become lifelong friends.

To the great assistant coaches with whom I spent so many hours in meeting rooms in Cedar Falls, Iowa; Madison, Wisconsin; Ames, Iowa; Indianapolis, Indiana; Oakland, California; Lincoln, Nebraska; Westwood, California; and Norman, Oklahoma. These assistant coaches are the lifeblood of football. It's staggering to think about the thousands of lives these men have affected in such life-changing ways. Thank you for your dedication and what you do for the players you coach and for this great game.

To all the great players I have coached, it has been my privilege to teach you and see you develop. I have always loved my guys, and there isn't a thing in the world I wouldn't do for any of you. It hasn't mattered to me if you were an all-American, a first-round draft choice, or a walk-on or free agent; if you respected the game and you laid it on the line for your teammates and coaches, you were one of my guys, and I would do anything for you. It's been my privilege and honor to coach each and every one of you.

To my father and mother, Merritt and Cynthia Norvell, all the great values that I know come from growing up under your roof. To Mom, thank you for always supporting me and being there for me through all the weekend games and late-night dinners. You were always there for me and my brother. Your love showed Aaron and me so much about loyalty and consistency. Dad, you always were the greatest example of leadership and sacrifice. You always showed me by your actions that the family and your obligations came first. My favorite memories are of you coaching my Little League baseball team. To this day you are my favorite coach. Thank you, Mom and Dad, for always being there for me and making my years growing up so special.

To my younger brother, Aaron, you have always supported me. My favorite years in coaching were when I was able to coach on the staff at

Wisconsin when my brother was finishing his last three years. I was the special-teams coordinator, and Aaron was by far my all-time favorite guy to coach. I still smile when I think of the big hits he had on our kickoff team. Nobody had more fun playing the game than my baby brother.

To my son, Jaden, I am trying to be the father that every kid deserves, because, Jaden, you deserve the best. You are so smart and talented in so many ways. My favorite time of the day is making breakfast and taking you to school. I am looking forward to watching you develop into the special young man I know you'll become.

To my wife, Kim, I could write an entire book on how unselfish and dedicated you have been to this family. People have no idea what it's like to be a coach's wife and take a family to different cities and make it all work, to handle all the day-to-day struggles by yourself while your husband is out chasing and worrying about a bunch of other 18- to 23-year-olds. Coaching is not a job; it is truly a lifestyle. From the start, Kim, you have been by my side. You have been the glue that has kept this family together and strong. You have been there for every professional move that has dragged us all over the United States. You have endured 24-game Super Bowl seasons and national championship seasons and all the recruiting weekends and the travel time I have been away. You have had to do so much on your own with no family support. I could live a thousand lifetimes and not be able to repay your sacrifice to this family, not to mention the love and support you have always given me and our players so we can chase our dreams. Thank you, you are the love of my life, and God has truly blessed me to have you to walk this journey by my side.

KEY TO DIAGRAMS

Offense

○	Offensive player
⊕	Center
QB	Quarterback
HB	Halfback
FB	Fullback
TB	Tailback
TE	Tight end
WR	Wide receiver

Defense

T	Defensive tackle
E	Defensive end
LB	Linebacker
M	Middle linebacker or Mike
S	Strongside linebacker or Sam
W	Weakside linebacker or Will
CB	Cornerback
DB	Defensive back
SS	Strong safety
FS	Free safety
CO	Coach
⟶	Run (solid line)
----▶	Pass (dashed line)
··········	Original alignment
⊢	Block
●—	Run and stop

1

A Receiver as a Weapon

In the sport of football, every position has a special place in the overall scheme of the game. A lineman does most of the dirty work, a lot of the heavy lifting. The offensive linemen's physical battles up front allow the rest of the offense to play. Everyone who enjoys the game must respect what the big guys do on the front lines. Their unselfish sacrifice and their battles in the trenches demonstrate the true essence of football.

The running backs advance the ball in a physically punishing manner. They must run the tough yards up the middle and also the speed plays on the outside around the flank of the defense. They also pass protect and pick up blitzing linebackers to allow the quarterback to make downfield throws. The running backs are the watchdogs who don't allow the quarterback to get hit when the defense sends an all-out blitz. This is an often overlooked but critical aspect of offensive execution.

The quarterback must communicate clearly and lead the offense with authority and confidence. He must get everyone on the same page. The quarterback is in charge of telling everyone what to do and reminding the team of the situation. The quarterback should be like another coach on the field, and the best ones are extensions of the coaching staff. A true field general must be a calm and composed leader in the heat of battle. In the chaos and pressure that occur when everything is going wrong and the opponent has the momentum—especially when playing in the frenzy of an opposing stadium—the quarterback must be the calming voice of reassurance that refocuses the team and gives them confidence. The quarterback's job is to distribute the ball to his playmakers and keep the offense on schedule and in rhythm. The bottom line is that the quarterback's job is to respect the football. He must move the team, leading them to score points, and he must operate the offense without making major mistakes. The quarterback's job is to win.

Last but not least are the receivers. Receivers are the perimeter weapons who attack the field both vertically and horizontally in the passing game. The receivers are often the most explosive and dynamic players on the field. In the NFL, we had a saying that no single player is more capable of changing the game in one play than the wide receiver. A receiver can strike like a lightning bolt out of nowhere and go for a 70-yard touchdown, totally changing the momentum of the football game. A complete receiver is the total package. The complete receiver not only is a great consistent playmaker as a ball catcher but also blocks on the perimeter in the run game and plays effectively without the ball in his hands. Wide receivers come in all shapes and sizes. Each wide receiver brings certain strengths and weaknesses to the team. Coaches will evaluate what type of weapon each receiver is for the team and how each receiver can best attack the defense.

> **"The will to win has been a dominating theme of the Raider organization. While no player has optimized that will more than Fred Biletnikoff, I will remember him most because he hated to lose."**
>
> *Oakland Raiders owner Al Davis on hall of fame receiver Fred Biletnikoff*

What Type of Weapon Are You?

I ask each player this question: What type of weapon are you? Each receiver brings different strengths and weaknesses to the game. How can you attack the defense? Is speed your advantage? Do you run great timing routes and catch the ball well in traffic? Do you have great size? Do you pose matchup problems for the defense in go-ball situations or in jump-ball situations in the red zone? There are many ways to be an effective wide receiver. Productivity is the key. Are you able to find a way to get the job done? That is the bottom line.

I compiled these ideas in 1990 when I was a young, idealistic coach. I was very passionate about my ideas, and I still am today.

Self-Assessment

What are your strengths? Is size one of your strengths? What are your height, weight, and build? Are you tall and lean, or are you short and muscular? Your body type affects how you will use your body as a weapon. Is speed your main strength? How fast are you? Do you have sprinter speed that lets you run past people (most players don't), or do you have average speed that requires you to be efficient and fundamentally sound to get open? Do you have functional speed that enables you to run past most defenders if you effectively set up the defender by using your head and proper fundamentals? How is your quickness? Are you super quick in and out of breaks with great body control? Do you make it almost impossible for defenders to get their hands on you because of your lateral quickness? Or do you have to use your head and a combination of hands and releases to get the job done?

Are you a stallion? A stallion has a higher level of pride than the other guy and sets higher expectations for himself. Coaches look for stallions.

What are your intangibles? Are you an intelligent student of the game? Playing smart is one of the most valuable qualities that any player can have. The best players are always looking for an edge. The best players are always challenging themselves to do the little things better than the other guy. Are you constantly studying how to do things better than your opponent? Are you aggressive? You must have an attacking nature to be great in sports. This game is won by guys who go after the prize. Action is the key to greatness in sports. Is that part of your personality? Do you like to compete? Are you a natural competitor? Do you want to win at everything you do? Some guys are just wired to fight for everything they can get. That is what the game of football was built on. Football is the most competitive game, and it attracts the most competitive men.

Do you want to be a football player? For the guys I grew up with, the greatest compliment that could be given to any player was that he was a football player, meaning that he played the game the way it was meant to be played. For example, Jerry Rice, Walter Payton, and Hines Ward are football players. These men played the game all out and did whatever they could do to help the team win. They were tougher than nails, and they were respected by everyone they played with and against.

Do you have a high motor? Is your mind active and are you always looking for the edge in every situation? Players with high motors play with a high level of energy and seem to outwork their opponents. They never rest! There is an old saying, "Good, better, best, I will never rest until my good gets better and my better is my best!"

How do you practice? First, are you on time? Are you punctual? Being early is even better. Being early is one of the highest forms of respect. I was lucky to work for Jim Mora Sr. for four years with the Indianapolis Colts. I love his belief about being early. He started every meeting about 5 minutes early, and once the players understood this, they were at every meeting— sitting and ready to go—at least 5 minutes early. Being early shows your teammates and coaches that you respect their time and that they have your attention.

Do you want to be special? I believe that you can tell a man's ultimate goal by the way he works every day. A man's everyday work ethic will tell you what he wants to accomplish in the long run. If a man wants to be uncommon and accomplish things that few men have done, then his everyday work effort will be uncommon. Michael Irvin would put on full pads and run routes full speed in the middle of the summer—well before training camp—because he wanted to be uncommon; he wanted to be the best. Jerry Rice used to train harder in February and March than most players would train all year. When most NFL players were on vacation or relaxing in the off-season, Rice was driving himself harder than ever. Why did he do this? Rice wanted to be not only the best receiver but also the best football player who had ever played the game.

How do you handle the little things? Great players are totally prepared because they work harder than everyone else and they are driven unlike the rest. The more experienced a player becomes, the more he realizes that his preparation is the key to his success. He knows that his preparation is what will give him the edge in competition.

Do you come to practice focused and ready to work? For a player, the 2-plus hours of practice should be his escape from the outside world. Every player must learn to drop all the baggage of the outside world before entering the locker room to prepare for practice. From the time practice starts until it is over, a player's total focus and concentration should be on the details of the specific practice.

Are you a detailed guy? Football has become very detailed and specific. The days of the dumb jock who can't spell *cat* if you spot him the *c* and the *t* are long gone. This is a game that must be played with intelligence and detail. Coaches are asking players to read and react in highly sophisticated ways that will challenge the players mentally. The difference between winning and losing will often be in the details. Therefore, to be effective, players, especially wide receivers, must be detail oriented. This has to become a part of their overall makeup. Today's modern passing game is built on the timing and precision of the quarterbacks. Receivers must be on the same page, and they must be able to make split-second decisions or adjustments to what they see at game speed. Sometimes thousands of details, both physical and mental, have to be handled properly to execute a pass play under the most competitive situations, such as third and 7 with the game on the line in the fourth quarter of the Super Bowl or the national championship.

Coach's Evaluation

At some point, coaches will look at you and evaluate what type of weapon you are.

Are you a consistent ball catcher? Receivers must be able to catch the ball in every situation. The receiver needs to be able to make the routine catch as well as the competitive play in traffic, each with consistency. This is the primary skill that defines the position. The athletic players who have ball skills become receivers at an early age. The athletic guys without great ball skills often end up on defense at an early age. There are exceptions; the very best defensive secondary players have great ball skills and could probably play on either side of the ball. Many great players could play on either side of the ball.

Can you go deep? One of the first things that a coach will evaluate is whether a player can stretch the field as a deep threat. If a player can do this, it opens up a lot of opportunities because he is always a threat to run by the defense. The defender knows in the back of his head that this player is capable of running past him, so the defender must always respect that. In turn, the defender may allow the receiver to have more room on short routes in fear of giving up a long pass to that receiver.

Will you compete and separate versus tight man coverage? I always tell my guys that a receiver must know what his job is. That job is as follows: first, to get open, and second, to catch the ball. The guy who can catch but can't get open will never be able to make plays versus tight coverage. The guy who can get open but cannot catch is not a dependable playmaker. So the ability to get open is a key to being an effective player.

Can you be counted on in the clutch when you are needed the most? When the team needs you to come through, can you make the play that will help the team win? It may be a routine play in space with nobody around, or it may be a tough play across the middle when you know you are going to take a big hit.

Are you tough minded? How will you respond when you are challenged? The physical nature of football makes it the most competitive game. Football is the only game in which somebody is knocked down on almost every play. So if you're playing the game, you are going to get knocked down. If you are playing the game, odds are you are going to get hurt at some point. How will you react when you get knocked down? The first drill that most players are taught in the game of football is up-downs or Lombardis. The first thing you better learn is to get back up and get in the fight. That's the essence of the game.

Are you a red-zone threat? Are you a big body who is mismatched in the red zone and can go up for jump balls and fades?

Are you a consistent route runner? Can you separate and do it consistently? Can you be counted on in the clutch to be precise and open on time? Can you get in and out of your cuts on double moves for big plays? It takes poise and intelligence to set up a defender on a double move. You must be a great actor and make the defender believe that you are doing one thing when in fact you are doing another. Often you will have only one chance in a game to use a double move on a defender. It may be something you saw on film, and you may have worked on setting up the play for weeks; in the game, you have only one chance to do it right. Poise, timing, and confidence all come into play to make this big play happen in the heat of the game.

Are you a willing blocker? The key word is *willing*. A football game will include an average of 72 plays. A great receiver may catch 10 to 12 passes in a big game. That leaves 60 plays during which the receiver doesn't get his hands on the football. Great players work hard for their team when they don't have the ball in their hands. That means they are willing blockers who play with great effort to help spring ballcarriers. Blocking is 10 percent technique and 90 percent "want-to"!

At the end of the day, the most important question is this: Can you be counted on to be a dependable playmaker whom your teammates can rely on in the clutch? Teams are built on trust. Your teammates must be able to trust that you are going to do your job.

Identity

You must also work to establish your identity as a football player. Your ultimate goal must be to reinforce your standing on a daily basis. Everyone gets a reputation. What will yours be? A good reputation isn't built overnight. Real respect as a player is built one day at a time. True excellence is reached through intelligence and dedication, and it is the mastery of the little things that will ultimately help you master the skills you need to be a consistent performer. Your identity will be formed by your discipline and the consistent habits you develop daily. As a young player, you will gain more opportunities by being prepared to take advantage of the ones you get. The better you perform, the more responsibility the coaches will give you. The ultimate goal must be to reinforce your reputation daily.

Your measure as a player will be established over blocks of time. You will be judged initially by a single play, then a drill, then a practice. Then you will be judged over a spring camp, a summer training camp, and a full season. Over the course of time, you will ultimately be judged based on your entire career. People will look back at all the qualities you had as a player and what type of legacy you will leave on the game and, more important, on the players who follow in your footsteps. What kind of example and mentor will you be for those players who follow in your footsteps?

Your coach will expect many things from you. Most important, the coach will want you to be a football player—the kind of guy who is hard nosed, hard playing, willing to sacrifice for the team, and always ready and willing to lay it on the line for his teammates. Every coach loves this kind of player. Football players don't complain; they seek challenges and hope that their number is called to be the one who has to make the play. Football players are reliable, consistent, and dependable—and most important, they are unselfish. The team is always more important than their own personal goals. They desire and strive to be a part of something bigger than themselves.

Types of Receivers

One of the things I love about football is that no matter what level you play at or where you are, people seem to remember what happens on the field. People remember what happens in games. Something about the physical nature of football is significant to people. It hits them in their core. It matters to them, and they remember. Maybe it's the respect people have for those who put themselves on the line and make sacrifices for such a physical game. People respect those who put themselves at risk. It is an admirable thing to put yourself in harm's way while the rest of the world sits on the sidelines and watches.

We had a saying about football in the National Football League: "It's not for everyone." Football is not for the weak of heart; you have to love it. Not everyone has the mental makeup to play football. Not everyone is mentally and physically wired to enter a battle of such physical contact. I believe that many people feel a special admiration for those who do battle on the gridiron. Whether it's a peewee football game, a college homecoming, or the NFL playoffs, every game has a special meaning to those who watch it. Because of that, what happens during the time you get to compete on the field will have a lasting effect on people who watch the game. That's the power of football.

Great receivers come in all shapes and sizes. Table 1.1 shows the measurements of some of the most productive receivers in NFL history as well as some of the top players in the 2011 NFL draft. These numbers show that effective players come with various body types.

Over the years, we have seen several big receivers. An example of a big receiver would be any player who is at least 6-foot-2 and close to 200 pounds. Terrell Owens, Randy Moss, Larry Fitzgerald, Dez Bryant, A.J. Green, and Julio Jones would all be categorized as big receivers. A big receiver has a physical advantage versus a smaller defensive back in a one-on-one situation. These players can really give the defense matchup problems. A big receiver gives smaller defensive backs problems because in man-to-man coverage, the size of the bigger, stronger receiver often allows him to make plays on balls even when the defender has good tight coverage. In effect, even when a big guy is covered, he still has the advantage one on one, and all the quarterback needs to do is throw the ball where the receiver has a chance to use his body and his physical advantage to make the play. An accurate throwing quarterback can exploit the defense and throw to a spot away from defenders to a big receiver. The physical advantage of the receiver really shows up on go balls and fade routes.

Speed receivers are known more for their ability to run and make people miss than for their size and strength. Jerry Rice was the most productive receiver in the history of the NFL, but the interesting thing is that Rice wasn't considered fast by NFL standards. Marvin Harrison was considered

TABLE 1.1 Measurements of Notable Receivers

	Height (feet, inches)	Weight (pounds)	40-yard dash (seconds)	Vertical jump (inches)	Broad jump (feet)
Jerry Rice	6'1.5"	196	4.6	32	na
Marvin Harrison	6'0"	181	4.31	34.5	10.2
Terrell Owens	6'2.7"	217	4.65	33	10
Randy Moss	6'3.6"	198	4.47	40	na
Chris Carter	6'1"	208	4.69	35	na
Steve Largent	5'11"	190	4.64	na	na
Tim Brown	6'0"	195	4.55	na	na
Keyshawn Johnson	6'3.3"	212	4.53	31.5	10.5
Hines Ward	5'1.5"	195	4.57	30.5	na
Isaac Bruce	5'11.4"	188	4.57	36.5	10.1
Steve Smith	5'9"	185	4.45	38.5	10.1
Wes Welker	5'8.7"	193	4.64	na	na
Larry Fitzgerald	6'3"	221	4.57	35	10.1
Anquan Boldin	6'0.6"	210	4.70	na	na
Reggie Wayne	6'0"	197	4.6	35	10
Chad Johnson	6'2"	198	4.58	33	9
Santana Moss	5'9.5"	185	4.38	42	10.4
Mark Clayton	5'10.3"	193	4.43	36.5	9.9
Percy Harvin	5'11.1"	192	4.42	37.5	10.1
Dez Bryant	6'2"	225	4.55	38	11.1
Julio Jones	6'2.6"	220	4.37	38.5	11.3
A.J. Green	6'3.5"	211	4.5	34.5	10.6

a speed receiver. He could really run, and any defender lining up on him had to be afraid of him running by the defender. That fear gave Harrison a great advantage because he could gain a nice cushion and separation on his intermediate routes. When Randy Moss came into the NFL, he was a unique combination of great size (almost 6-foot-4) and blazing speed (a 4.47-second 40-yard dash). Plus, he was so rangy that it was almost impossible to overthrow him on a deep ball. He did things on a football field that no man had ever done with his kind of consistency. I have seen him run a post route versus Cover 2, and when he got about 7 yards away from the safety, Moss threw his hand up in the air to signal the quarterback. This signal indicated that Moss was about to run right past the safety and that the quarterback should throw the ball to him as far as he possibly could. Throwing post routes into Cover 2 is a "no" for any trained quarterback at the higher levels of football because Cover 2 is truly double coverage. The great physical talents of a young Randy Moss with the Vikings blew away that conventional thinking. It was an incredible thing to see. He was so fast and his strides were so long that at the 15-yard mark he had built up a full stride length, and I don't know if there was a man in the world who could keep up with him at that point. In addition, his arms were so long that he could run the deep ball down in full stride and pluck it without slowing down, making it almost impossible to cover.

Jerry Rice ran a 4.6 40-yard dash, which by NFL standards is not considered fast. But Rice rarely got caught on the field. Jerry Rice caught 197 touchdown passes, more than any other player in the history of professional football (table 1.2). This is one of the most hallowed records in sports. Interesting enough, Terrell Owens (with Randy Moss) is second all-time at 153. Rice has the yardage record of 22,895 for a career; Terrell Owens is second at 15,934. Owens is quite a way from Rice on both records, which shows you the greatness of Jerry Rice. But it's interesting that the two most productive receivers in NFL history ran the 40-yard dash at 4.6 and 4.65, respectively, both slow by NFL standards. Rice has the record for career receptions with 1,549; Marvin Harrison is number 2 with 1,102. Harrison would be considered a speed receiver, running a blazing 4.31 40-yard dash at the combine. Harrison also has the record for most catches in an NFL season with 148 in 2002. In addition, Harrison has the record for most receptions in a two-year period (252) in 2001 and 2002.

What is a stallion? If you have ever been to a racetrack and witnessed the power and grace of a great race horse, you know what a stallion is. The stallion is strong, powerful, and simply the most impressive physical specimen on the field. The stallion knows he is good and carries himself with supreme confidence. The stallion has courage and supreme stamina. The stallion will run all day. He is a bundle of pure physical energy, power, and grace. Great receivers don't want to come out of the game. Great receivers want to catch every ball in practice. Great receivers are different from the rest. They have the ability to push themselves a little harder when the others get tired. The stallion has a champion's heart and will push himself to do his job. He wants to be the one who makes the crucial play. The stallion gets it. He knows what his job is and what his role is for the offense. He wants the responsibility of being the go-to guy when the team needs it most. He relishes that opportunity. To him it isn't pressure, it's what makes him a player.

TABLE 1.2 NFL Receiving Records Held by Jerry Rice

	Rice	Next closest wide receiver
Receiving touchdowns	197	153 (Terrell Owens and Randy Moss)
Receiving yards	22,895	15,934 (Terrell Owens)
Receptions	1,549	1,102 (Marvin Harrison)

Qualities of Wide Receivers

To play wide receiver well, a player must possess a combination of physical traits. Body control and agility are essential to a receiver's success. The primary thing that a receiver must have is the ability to adjust. Anyone can run a 12-yard pass route against air and turn around. The real challenge comes when the receiver faces a defender who is one of the best athletes on the field and who is using the bump-and-run technique.

A receiver must be able to avoid obstacles and move his body in space. To be able to adjust, a player must have a high level of agility. This is the ability to change body position—even in midair—to make a critical play. Upper-body flexibility is also an important part of body control. Upper-body flexibility is the ability to get the hands in position to catch balls that are thrown behind the receiver or thrown poorly. One of the most important aspects of being able to catch the ball is getting the body in position so the ball can be caught. Upper-body flexibility allows the hands to get into place to make the difficult play. This is one of the most fundamental but least understood skills of receiver play, but it is so obvious when you see a smooth, natural athlete with great ball skills pluck a difficult ball out of the air and make it look easy.

Strength is also very important for a receiver. Strength can help in many ways. It helps players get off the line when the defensive back tries to jam them. Strength helps when two players are fighting for position as they run down the field and work for position on the ball. Strength also helps when going up for high balls and jump balls. Plus, adding strength will help players take the pounding and rigors of a long season. Players who are very productive for a long time, such as Jerry Rice and Terrell Owens, have great conditioning and a high level of body strength.

Having sure, soft hands, especially the ability to catch the ball in crowded situations, is the skill that defines the receiver position. As players move up in levels of competition, catches become more competitive. The biggest difference between college football and pro football is defense. The NFL is full of the greatest, smartest defensive athletes in the world, and the coverage in pro football is so good that nearly every ball is a contested ball. That's why the quarterbacks have to be so accurate at that level, because the coverage is so good. Most receivers can run under a pass and catch it, but it takes a truly special player to be able to consistently catch the ball in crowded situations. The ability to catch the ball while being simultaneously hit is the measuring stick for sure hands.

Great focus is the ability to block out all distractions and have single-minded concentration on the football. It's the ability to block out the crowd, the defenders, and the elements in order to keep all the focus on the football to make the play. Great focus is the ability to know that you are going to be hit but still keep your critical attention on the ball. Focus is the ability to see the ball, feel the sideline, and then make the catch while simultaneously getting your toes down before you get out of bounds.

A good wide receiver is able to find open spaces. The wide receiver's job is to bring the playbook alive. Every route in the playbook has a certain depth and spacing on the field. The receiver's job is to run the route at the proper depth and get open at the proper time. The playbook is full of plays, but the skill and discipline of the receiver brings the playbook and the passing game to life. The football field is 120 yards long from endline to endline. Each field is 53 1/3 yards wide. The wide receiver needs to dissect that field and find the open spaces in the zones of the defense. Seeing the space in the coverage, running to it, and sitting down in it are what route running is all about. Smart players who understand coverage and have the best feel for sitting in space are the ones who catch the most balls. Marvin Harrison had a great feel for space. Ryan Broyles (who plays for Oklahoma) has an incredible knack for feeling the space in the zone as well. Both of these players have great peripheral vision and are able to see holes in the defenders' positioning that the average player doesn't see. This is a learned skill that has a lot to do with a player's vision and intelligence, as well as a real understanding of defensive coverage and structure.

Speed and acceleration are also key. Although 100-meter speed is desirable, separation speed is most effective on the football field. Functional speed is what a player uses when he breaks into the open field and runs away from people. We've seen many players who would not win the sprint at a track meet but are able to break out in the open with the ball in their hands and never get caught. This competitive speed, or functional speed, matters the most on the football field. Jerry Rice is probably the most famous player who didn't have a particularly fast 40-yard dash time (4.6 seconds, which is average by NFL standards). However, Rice was the most productive receiver in NFL history. Even late in his career, when I was with Jerry Rice and the Oakland Raiders in 2002, he would catch the ball on the run in the open field and run away from most NFL defensive backs. He just had incredible competitive speed in the open field. Often this results from not only having the ability to run fast but also knowing where to run in the context of a football play. This separates the player with real football sense from those who don't have it.

"I was the first one out to practice. I worked my butt off. I was in such great shape they wanted to catch me, they tried to catch me, but they couldn't catch me."

Hall of famer Jerry Rice

Coachability is the willingness of a player to learn, and it's a huge factor in a player's overall success. Players who want to learn will improve faster, no matter what level they are at. It's an attitude they carry with them. There is a saying in the NFL that the best players want to be coached. That is true of the very best players I have been around. The great ones love to be coached because they are always looking for ways to be the very best.

It is also true that the harder you work, the faster you improve as a player. Those who listen and work hard are the ones who improve the fastest. The greatest example of this for me, although he isn't a wide receiver, is Peyton Manning. We drafted Peyton out of Tennessee in 1998 with the number 1 pick. In the first eight games of his rookie year with the Indianapolis Colts, Peyton was terrible, making a lot of mistakes and throwing a ton of interceptions. In the second half of the season, it was amazing to see the transformation in this kid and what he became as a player. His improvement was incredible because the kid worked his tail off to get better every day. Plus, he studied and learned from his mistakes. In the second half of his rookie season, he became a different player. I have never seen a player improve as fast at such a difficult position as Peyton Manning did his rookie season.

Like all good players, a wide receiver needs to have durability. I compare receivers to foreign sports cars. The good ones are highly tuned machines. They often have to be almost completely healthy to perform at a high level. Unlike other positions, most receivers have a difficult time performing when injured. Any NFL player who has played for a number of years has had to play through an assortment of pain and injuries to stay productive over time. The average fan has no idea what professional players go through every week to play on Sundays. Ryan Broyles is the best I've been around at the college level at playing with and through injury. He has played in some of the biggest games with shoulder, ankle, and foot injuries that would have kept most players on the sidelines.

The great ones "need to eat." I have had the opportunity to coach some great record-setting players both in college and in the NFL. They all have different strengths and weaknesses, but amazingly, they have much in common. The great ones are all extremely smart and highly competitive. The other quality that the great player has is an undeniable hunger for the football. He never gets tired of making plays. He always wants the ball. He needs the ball like he needs to eat, like he needs to breathe. He always wants more and is ready to make the next play. You can't feed him enough. He has this hunger for the ball that comes from the confidence of making plays over and over. It's not a selfish thing; it's an undeniable craving for making plays. The thing about receivers, they can't do their job without help from the quarterback and the play caller, and receivers who want the ball will always let the quarterback and play caller know about it.

The best players are almost always very smart and quick minded. Slow thinkers with poor awareness don't make great receivers. The great receivers are always able to see two steps ahead. They are great anticipators of the landscape around them. They are quick minded and have the ability to adjust with the moving parts of an ever-flowing game. The modern passing game is a chess game, and the parts are always moving. Receivers and quarterbacks must constantly be ready to adjust and apply certain routes and patterns in order to attack the constantly changing coverages that defenses throw at them. Even more important, the quarterback and the receivers must think alike and be on the same page.

Some people don't think of receivers as being tough. It takes a different kind of mental toughness and courage to run across the middle of the field on third and 10 and stretch out for a crossing route when you know you're going to get hit. It takes toughness to crack a linebacker who weighs 30 to 40 pounds more than you on a pitch play. It takes toughness to dig out a safety on a stretch play so he doesn't tackle the running back. It takes toughness to consistently catch the ball on short intermediate passes across the middle and take hits from linebackers and safeties. A guy such as Wes Welker of the New England Patriots is tough because he catches the ball in the middle in traffic, and he has the courage to run these routes time and time again when the linebackers would love to take him out. Steve Largent was a hall of fame player for the Seattle Seahawks. In a famous play, Largent was hit and knocked out of the opening game of the season by Denver Broncos safety Mike Harden. Fourteen games later that season, the Seahawks were again playing the Denver Broncos, and Mike Harden intercepted the ball in the Seahawks' end zone and began to return it across the field. As Harden crossed the field, Largent flew out of nowhere and laid the safety out cold. It was one of the greatest retribution hits in NFL history and a great example of a hall of famer's pride and toughness! Steve Largent had a great comment about his ability. He wasn't all that big or fast, but he is in the hall of fame because of the way he competed. He said, "I would compete just as hard at the beginning as I would at the end," meaning the beginning of a play, series, or game. Great players go after and compete for the ball from the beginning all the way to the end. Hines Ward of the Pittsburgh Steelers, one of my favorite players, plays so hard and unselfishly without the ball that it inspires everyone around him. He is a joy to watch because he will do anything to help his team win. He will sacrifice his body, and some of his hits on opposing defenders would make a great highlight reel. Hines Ward is a great example of how to play the game hard and tough. He is the ultimate team player and champion.

"Without toughness, dedication, and heart, without the will to persevere, all the skill in the world won't make you a winner."

Bill Parcells in Finding a Way to Win:
The Principles of Leadership, Teamwork, and Motivation

Thoroughbreds are temperamental. I don't know why, but the best receivers seem to carry some of the same personality traits as thoroughbreds. They seem to crave attention, they love the limelight, and they are a little temperamental and moody at times. They are definitely high strung. The very best ones take some maintenance, and it just seems to come with the package. I won't get personal here, but if you do the research, you'll learn that highly successful wide receivers love to be the center of attention. I don't think this comes from being selfish as much as it does from these players wanting to do their job well and help the team. To do that, they believe that they have to catch the ball and make big plays, so they want it in the worst way. The great ones are used to making plays, and if they go too long without the ball, they are sure to tell people about it. I have come to expect this from the very best receivers. They need to eat, and the coach has to feed them with the ball to keep them satisfied. Marvin Harrison used to rub his belly every time he wanted the ball as a reminder to the coaching staff that he hadn't had it for a while. That has become a universal symbol for those in the receiver community. I have never been around a great receiver who didn't want the ball as often as possible.

"The first quality that makes an athlete a winner is simply pride. He has such a desire to excel he will take enormous pains. He will work out beyond what is demanded, build his body during the off-season, guard his weight, and study the problems of his position. The second quality is toughness, doing what the job requires without worrying about the physical consequences. A wide receiver will make the catch untroubled by the possibility of getting blindsided. The winning player has no fear in doing what must be done in order to be great."

Former Oakland Raiders coach John Madden

Great receivers have pride and a strong work ethic. It is one thing to have great physical ability that enables you to run and catch successfully, but to have a great career in which you are productive over time, you must have the character that stands the test of time. You can't be truly special—you can't be the best at your position—without great pride and tremendous work ethic. Pride is that inner competitiveness that says, "I want to be the best, not only the best on my team but better than anyone I play against." If you're truly special, you want to be better than anyone who has ever played. Not many players can realistically take that mind-set, although I have been around some who could. But whatever level you play at—high school, college, or pro—you have to play with the utmost confidence. Playing with confidence means that you walk on the field believing that you are going to play better than everyone else on the field—believing that you cannot be covered and that you will not be stopped. Not today.

Summary

I have spent a quarter century studying the physical and mental qualities of great receivers. A great receiver is such a complicated combination of traits—agility, body control, strength, quickness, soft hands, physical stamina, concentration, focus, toughness, pride, eye–hand coordination, vision, intelligence, the ability to conceptualize concepts. I could go on. This list still doesn't seem to paint the total picture of what makes a great player. Exceptional playmakers are made of something special. They have great ability to control their body, and they have an uncanny ability to make plays on the football that others can only dream of. Their pride and competitiveness are at another level than the rest. The complete receiver is one of the most incredible things to view in sports because he can do things we all wish we could do. It is a beautiful and exciting thing to watch. In the next chapter, we will examine how great players refine their game in practice.

2
Practice

Let's talk about practice. Basketball guard Allen Iverson of the Philadelphia 76ers had the classic reaction "We are talking about practice" when reporters questioned him about practice. He famously questioned the importance of practice. Of course, Iverson was one of the great point guards in the NBA; in hindsight, I don't think these were his true feelings about practice. He didn't get to be an MVP of the NBA by not practicing.

In this chapter, we look at the important aspects of how to practice. When it comes to ensuring that you perform at your best, practice is everything. The best practices are purposeful and filled with enthusiasm. The old saying is that practice makes perfect; we like to think that perfect practice makes perfect. The simple fact is that not much in football ends up being perfect, and things often don't have to be perfect to be counted as a win. But for your skill level to be exceptional, you must have principles to live by. The closer to perfect you are, the better your chances of winning will be.

Punctuality

Be on time. Whether it is the beginning of practice or a meeting, you should be on time. Being 5 to 10 minutes early is even better. We have a saying that if you are there 5 minutes early, waiting for the practice or meeting to start, then you are on time. You don't want to walk in just as practice is starting. You certainly don't want to walk in after practice has begun, because this shows a total disrespect for your teammates and coaches.

At some levels, a football team may have 80 to 100 players. When a player walks in late, he is wasting the time of all the members of the team. Jim Mora Sr., former coach of the Indianapolis Colts, was a stickler for being on time. He would start every team meeting 5 to 10 minutes early. Punctuality was about the player's individual accountability. The same goes for practice. Being ready to go on time for practice shows that you are accountable to your coaches and teammates. It is a sign of respect, and it shows that the team goals and practice are important to you. Being on time and ready to go is the first step to having a great practice.

Attitude

First, your attitude must be upbeat. You want to be an open book, someone who is there to get something accomplished. Every practice has a purpose. Coaches spend a lot of time detailing what they want to get from each practice. You must know the purpose of each practice and work to get those goals accomplished. Good players are on the same page with their coaches. Good players know why they are working on something, and they stay on task. Experienced players on winning teams understand the importance of practicing at a high level. They have seen that teams win championships when they do things right in practice. Bringing that attitude to practice will rub off on the younger players.

"I'm a great believer in luck, and I find the harder I work, the more of it I have."

Thomas Jefferson

To listen is to be silent. A good friend once pointed out to me that if you rearrange the letters in *listen,* you make the word *silent.* In short, you can't listen unless you are first silent. As a player, when the coach is talking, you should keep your mouth closed and be quiet. The old saying that "coaches coach, players play, and administrators administrate" is true. Whenever a coach is correcting any player, you should pay attention; you may not have made the mistake this time, but paying attention could save you from making the same mistake in the future. You want to take advantage of every opportunity to learn, so you should always pay close attention to any coaching point.

Energy

I can't overemphasize the importance of energy in making a good practice. I love football. I have always loved football. Every day is a great day when I can be on a practice field and practice. I have always brought that outlook to the field. I love the games, but to me practice is equally important. Practice is everything because in the end you will perform how you practice. As a player, I never looked at practice any differently than the games. I played at the same speed in practice as I did in the games. There was no difference to me.

Coaches must understand how their energy and enthusiasm set the tempo and the atmosphere for practice. The energy of coaches is infectious on the practice field. It lifts everyone's focus and energy. Upbeat, positive coaches give players energy. Dark and heavy coaches zap the energy of players and coaches alike. Coaches have to realize how important it is to be upbeat and energetic on the field. This is especially important after a tough loss. After a loss, players may be downbeat and carrying the loss like a heavy burden. This takes away from their energy. The best thing a coach can do when a team has had a tough loss is to come out upbeat and ready to work. This will help the players get that loss out of their system and will help get the team back on track.

Intensity

Players must learn to compete every day in every way. Football is the most competitive game, and it is played by the most competitive men. To get players to play this game at the highest level, the great coaches create the most competitive environment every day in practice. The player must bring himself to this environment every day and develop a mind-set that enables him to compete in every way. You should learn to compete in everything you do on a football field because that is what you need to do on game day. You must bring this competitive mind-set to the practice field every day.

"Don't mistake activity for achievement; practice it the right way."

John Wooden, hall of fame basketball coach for UCLA

Work with an edge. When you are practicing a certain skill, you must do it properly. You gain nothing by working on the skill at 50 percent of what you will use in a game. You must practice skills at game speed, game tempo, and game effort or you won't really know if you have performed the skills properly. Whether you are working on releases, hand drills, or routes, you better bring it with effort and intensity or you're wasting a lot of time (unless your plan is to play your games at half or three-quarter speed).

I like to call it working with an edge. The best players get it. Once it becomes a habit, a player can play and win at a high level. It is the biggest edge in competitive sports. The work is the competitive edge. Players become what they do over and over. People say that you have to do something for 17 days before it becomes a habit. Players rely on that muscle memory in those great competitive moments on the field. They need to learn to love the work, embrace it, and recognize that repetition leads to winning. Once they learn this, they must never forget.

The football gods love to remind us when we don't put in the necessary work. A player's preparation will always show up in his performance on game day. Working with an edge is what coaches spend their lives in this game doing. This is a learned process that players must experience for themselves. They have to see how the hours of preparation and repetition make the difference on game day.

> **"People perform most reliably when they're sure they can handle the task at hand, and that sureness comes only with specific preparation."**
>
> *Bill Parcells*

Grading Success

As a coach, I make it a habit of grading players in practice as much as I can, especially in early-season practices or in spring practice (at the college level). Players have to know what is expected of them and what is not. They have to know what a winning effort is and what is not acceptable.

I like to keep it very simple. You have a job to do on every play. You either did your job or you didn't, plus or minus. The measurement is a winning performance. Did you make the catch? Did you block your man? Did you effectively execute what we are teaching? Is it good enough to win? The coaches can find out in a hurry which players are doing what they are supposed to be doing. It's so easy to show the players what they need to do to improve. For me, 85 percent is the standard of a winning performance. Anything below that isn't good enough for the player to play on the field in the fall. Grading sets the standard, a level of play that a player needs to achieve while he is on the field. You must practice with a purpose. That purpose is to play with the highest skill level possible and to bring a winning performance to your play on a consistent, daily basis.

Reputation

Tom Moore, the great long-time offensive coordinator with the Indianapolis Colts, used to tell his players, "Everyone gets a reputation. What will yours be?" There has never been a truer statement. After a certain amount of time, people will form an opinion of you. What will they say about you? Are you a hard worker? Do you hustle? Are you a detailed player? Do you want to be a great player? Will you go the extra mile for your teammates? Do you know your assignments? Are you a team guy, or are you a selfish player who is always looking out for what's in it for you? Do you want to win a championship? Are you tough minded? Will you play through pain? Are you willing to sacrifice for your teammates? Are you coachable?

Everyone gets a reputation. You have to protect yours with your life. It's one of the most important things you have. Protect your reputation with all you have because once you get one, good or bad, it's difficult to shake it. You have to know what you want people to say about you before you ever step out on the practice field. Everything you do on that field will form your reputation. Protect your reputation. Once your reputation is formed, changing people's minds about you will be twice as difficult. Once you get a good reputation, people will often think of you based on that reputation before they even see you play. That's the power of reputation.

I grew up watching the Big Red Machine, the Cincinnati Reds baseball dynasty. They were world champions, and one of their great players was a guy named Pete Rose. Although he was a smaller player, Rose was a scrappy, rugged, switch-hitting dynamo. Pete Rose was an overachieving, hard playing ballplayer who was known for his headfirst slides on the basepaths. He would run as hard as he could on every play. For that reason, Pete Rose became known throughout the sports world by his nickname Charlie Hustle. It was as well earned as any nickname, and it thoroughly described how Rose played the game. He played all out. Perhaps the greatest compliment a ballplayer can be given is a nickname like Charlie Hustle.

Pete Rose was a hard playing and overachieving ballplayer with a reputation for hard work. He once said that he took 100 ground balls before every game and took early batting practice whenever he could. He was always challenging himself. He would work on his reflexes by having the pitcher at batting practice throw as hard as he could from 45 feet away. To Rose, it didn't matter where he played, whether it was the minor leagues or the big leagues, because he played with pride.

In my two years with the Oakland Raiders, Jerry Rice had already established his hall of fame career. Many players called him the Goat. After a while, I found out that *goat* was short for "greatest of all time." In most instances, this would seem like an overstatement or exaggeration, but in Rice's case, the nickname was accurate.

These are examples of two giants of American sports and how their reputations formed their nicknames. Pete Rose was given another nickname at the end of his career. He was known as the Hit King after getting more than 4,000 hits and breaking the all-time record for hits in a major-league career. These two sport icons—one is the all-time hit king in baseball and the other owns every major receiving record in the NFL—were both tagged with nicknames earned by their reputations as hardworking players.

Breakthroughs

Every player should come to practice every day and strive to break through in areas where he needs to improve. A player should be constantly working to break through in areas that will make him perform on a higher level. It may be a specific fundamental such as timing on a route. It may be reading a certain coverage or beating a certain technique. For productive practices to take place, a player must achieve a breakthrough in some area every day. A breakthrough means improvement. Players will continue to work hard when they constantly see that they are getting better.

Relationships

Because the passing game takes trust, the quarterback–receiver relationship is key. Trust is developed over time and repetitions. Peyton Manning and Marvin Harrison understood this. In every down minute during practice, Manning was throwing a timing route to Harrison. It was a constant every practice. Peyton threw to Marvin for hours. Game days with the Colts in those early years were amazing. Peyton Manning, Marvin Harrison, and Edgerrin James would put some shorts on and go out on the field to throw routes for 35 to 40 minutes every week before the team would go out to warm up. It was amazing to see. It was as if they were getting an entire extra practice in, one more than their opponents did. Those three players had such a connection together. They were the best players at their positions in the league for those years, and a lot of it had to do with the extra time they spent working together. The relationship that a receiver and a quarterback build together can only be developed over time and endless repetitions.

The quarterback–receiver relationship is a unique one. Often the quarterbacks and receivers are very different types of people, and even though they like each other, they don't hang out together much off the field. But over the years, I have seen some incredible similarities among all the great quarterback–receiver combinations that I have been around. The first thing is that they constantly talk to one another about what they see. The great quarterback and receiver are always working to get on the same page about coverages and discussing what they are going to do if various scenarios arise. Manning and Harrison were like that. Gannon and Rice were always talking to each other about what they saw from the defense.

The great players always spent extra time together in practice, throwing the route until it was absolutely right. Manning and Harrison would throw the same route over and over and over again.

The final element of the quarterback–receiver relationship is somewhat strange but very consistent among the great players. No matter what their relationship is during the week (in some cases, they might never be together except in practice), on the night before the game and on game day, the best quarterback and receiver are usually almost inseparable. They are almost always together in meetings, at dinner, at snacks. They can be seen everywhere together. It is the strangest thing, but it has happened on every good team I have ever been associated with. The great quarterback and receiver just seem to find each other as it gets closer to game time.

Execution

A great player is willing to do what is required for a great performance. There is a huge difference between putting in time and doing what is required for a great performance. Great players know that there are no shortcuts to doing things right. You must do what is required to be ready to play great. If that means practicing the same footwork over and over again until it is right, then that's what you must do. If that means running the same play five or six times until the timing is just right, then that is what's required. Most players and most teams are willing to put time into practice, but few are willing to do what is truly required to prepare to play great. That's why there is only one championship team every year—because it's difficult to make the sacrifices involved in doing what is required to play great.

Execution builds trust. In the heat of battle, both good and bad things happen. Under the pressure of the game when it counts most, players must be able to trust each other. As a player, you need to know that the guy next to you has paid the price and that you can count on him to do his job when the chips are down. This is especially true in the passing game. In critical situations, the quarterback will look for his most dependable receivers—guys who will come through in the toughest situations. This trust can be developed only through endless repetitions.

Football players may experience two types of pain: the pain of discipline and the pain of regret. The pain of discipline is the everyday toil of running routes, running sprints, doing all your conditioning work, staying after practice, and catching extra balls. This is difficult and painful.

The pain of discipline is small compared to the pain of regret after losing a big game because you didn't put in the required time and work in practice to be totally prepared for the game. The pain of regret is much worse, and it stays with you forever. The pain of discipline is only temporary.

Responsibility

Ask questions but don't slow down practice. If you don't understand something, be sure to ask. At the college level, coaches are meticulous about covering most questions in meetings and walk-throughs; however, if you have questions, you should ask them. You must also pay attention and learn from the mistakes of other players. We tell players that if a coach makes a correction for one player in practice, all the players are responsible for knowing that correction. You must learn to think on your feet and learn on the run, because that's the way it happens in the game.

Physicality

Football is and always will be a physical game. Players must bring a physical mentality to practice. Not every practice will be a scrimmage. Many aspects of football take footwork and timing and don't involve a lot of banging. But there is a time and a place for banging in practice, and when the time comes, you need to have an appetite for the physicality of the game. This is essential to success in football.

Teams and players who are physical and tough mentally will win consistently. If players are used to practicing tough and physically, they will play tough and physically. Iron sharpens iron. You have to compete your hardest every day to be at your best on game day, and this is as much mental as it is physical.

Some head coaches believe in having more physical padded practices than others. I believe that the way you practice and work becomes a part of your makeup. It becomes how you identify yourself, how you see yourself, your temperament, and your reputation. Football is physical and competitive. The places where I have coached have all had physical and competitive practices, and those practices help form the mentality of the players and the team. The mental toughness is just as important as the physical toughness.

Special Teams

Coaches expect every player to contribute in some fashion on special teams. The kicking game is often the difference between winning and losing, and players have to understand the importance of these phases of the game. The best players and the backups must all have some role in the kicking game. As a return man, a cover guy, or a blocker on a kickoff or punt return, a receiver can make an impact on special teams.

Habits

Do it right the first time to build the right habits. The saying in coaching is "do it wrong and do it long," which is another way of saying you should do it right the first time. For example, if players aren't focused or executing properly, a head coach will often have them repeat the drill from the start. Bill Belichick has not been afraid to take this to the extreme. If he doesn't see focus, he has been known to start practice all over again from scratch. If the practice is really bad, he may even require the players to go back in the locker room, get taped and dressed again, and repeat the whole practice. Coach Belichick is very determined to get a focused practice one way or another.

"We never do anything well until we cease to think about it."

William Hazlitt, 1778-1830

The Laws of Learning

John Wooden, the legendary UCLA basketball coach, is considered to be the greatest coach of all time. He built a basketball dynasty at UCLA during which he won 10 national championships. Coach Wooden had a great reputation for his ability as a teacher. At the height of UCLA's success, their offensive execution was far superior to the rest of college basketball. Their philosophy was that they just wanted to run their offense. To do this effectively, the team concentrated on the four laws of learning. They didn't really care who the opponent was; they were just going to execute what they had done in practice over and over again.

As Wooden wrote in his book *Wooden*, the four laws of learning are explanation, demonstration, imitation, and repetition. You want to create a correct habit so that you perform it instinctively when under pressure. This leads to an expansion of the laws of learning from four to eight: explanation, demonstration, imitation, repetition, repetition, repetition, repetition, and repetition.

When I was 12 years old, I entered a local basketball contest called Shoot, Pass, and Dribble. This competition tested your basketball fundamentals, and one test was to shoot free throws. My father challenged me that if I wanted to win, I had to practice hard and invest time in my preparation. We had a hoop over our garage, and I practiced night and day, especially free throws, in the weeks leading up to the competition. When the competition came, I was very confident. I stood at the free-throw line and knocked down those free throws. I won because I prepared so hard and was ready to use the skills I practiced when I was called on to perform.

You need to work through the rough spots. Some practices, especially early practices, won't be perfect. For players and coaches, some of the greatest strides are made in later practices. Don't let frustration overtake you and prevent you from experiencing the benefit of these later breakthroughs. As much as we try to make the game perfect, football is an unperfected sport. Sometimes you have to work through the rough spots to find improvement.

Norvell's Eight Suggestions for Success

1. Players must respect the opportunity to play by preparing to be their best.
2. Players should never care about their opponent. They should care about their own play.
3. The difference is in the details.
4. Hustle makes up for many mistakes.
5. A player must simply focus.
6. Critical self-analysis is important for improvement.
7. The one who plays the hardest the longest wins.
8. In the end, the most prepared and tough-minded team wins.

The Last Guy off the Field

Players who do more work seem to play better. I have always been interested in observing what happens on the practice field after practice. Some players stay after practice to do some extra work. Some coaches and players take advantage of the extra time to work on fundamentals that they didn't get enough work on during practice. It's amazing when you take note of which players are the last ones on the field. Many of the very best players are often the last ones to leave the practice field. Long after most guys are showered and are eating dinner, some guys are still on the field working—working until it's done right; that's what great players do. They know that there is always someone else out there trying to outwork them. To be at the top of your game, you have to put in extra time. For me, one of the great images of football is the picture of a couple of players on an empty practice field long after everyone is gone.

"I stay after practice to catch passes. I look at myself as encouragement to the common man who doesn't have great speed. If you work hard too, you can make it."

Steve Largent, hall of fame receiver for the Seattle Seahawks

At the end of the day, playing well at any level comes down to confidence. Doing things well in practice gives players the confidence to do things well in game situations. That confidence can be gained only from simulating what happens on game day. True competitive confidence comes from having success on game day. The ultimate goal is for a player to have the mind-set that on game day he can make the critical play when he needs to the most. To be more confident at game time, a player needs to perform as many pressure-packed, gamelike repetitions as possible in practice. The best athletic programs at any level are those where the player says that the game was easier than practice. In those programs, the players really look forward to game day because that's where the real fun is. I have always told players that as coaches our hardest work is done during the week. Game day is the player's time to shine!

Practice With Purpose

- Come ready to work. Concentrate and focus all your mental energy on the task at hand.
- Practice with a gamelike tempo. If game tempo is level 10, practice at 8 or 9. You can't practice at level 3 and expect to turn it up on game day.

- Practice with an edge. Working with intensity and purpose will bring functional efficiency to your skills.
- Strive to break through.
- Execute in areas that require effort (blocking downfield, running after the catch). Get into the good habit of finishing every play. A man's ultimate goals show up in his daily work.
- Be physical. Football is a physical game.
- Be attentive. Learn from the mistakes of other players.
- If you have a question, ask. However, keep in mind that coaches will not constantly remind you of your responsibilities on the field. You must invest time in learning what to do.
- Jump in and help out on scouting teams. Make yourself and your teammates better.
- Dedicate yourself to being a complete player
- Contribute in the kicking game. Every player can have some type of role on special teams.
- Work on skills after practice.
- Remember Wooden's eight laws of learning: explanation, demonstration, imitation, repetition, repetition, repetition, repetition, repetition.
- Remember that practice is never over until it's over. Don't let mistakes made early in practice affect strides that can be made later in practice.

Effective Practice

Here are the building blocks of an effective practice structure:

- **Walk-through** (10 to 15 minutes): On work days in training camp and spring practice, we typically have a 10- to 15-minute walk-through before the stretch. During a walk-through, the coach can introduce new concepts, and the offense can run new plays before running them in practice. The walk-through is an opportunity to get another repetition at a new concept. An offense will often run the same concepts but will window-dress them by using different formations or will disguise them by using certain shifts. The walk-through is a perfect opportunity to introduce these new formations or movements. Players don't walk through a walk-through. They usually go at 75 to 80 percent speed, which is more of a teaching tempo. Players should not have big collisions, receivers should not dive for footballs, and quarterbacks shouldn't launch deep balls that require receivers to open up and run full speed. The walk-through occurs before the team stretch, and the purpose is to teach. Full-speed running isn't emphasized. Players are not loose yet and haven't had the opportunity to stretch, so running full speed at this point in practice may put players in jeopardy for pulled muscles.

•   **Stretch** (10 minutes): The stretch typically lasts about 10 minutes. During this time, the players limber up their entire body. The players must get the body warmed up and ready for a full-speed practice. Players need to get the legs and hamstrings loose so the players can open up and run. They also want to get the back and groin loose in order to get the whole body ready for more intense work. Active stretching has become very popular. Agilities are introduced at the beginning of the stretch to get the players' blood flowing to the muscles, which allows the muscles to get loose quicker.

•   **Individual drills** (15 to 20 minutes): The next section of practice is for individual drills. For the overall practice, the concept is to practice as individual parts, then groups, and then the whole team. Players work at the individual parts of the skills, then work in smaller groups, and then work with the entire 11 players on offense. The first phase is the individual period. During this period, players split up based on individual position and work on position-specific drills that help them to execute the system or plays that will be run in practice that day. Coaches have to make sure that every drill has a specific purpose. A coach may emphasize certain drills on certain days. The coach should make sure that the drills simulate exactly what happens in a live game. The big mistake that some coaches make is that they copy drills and don't really have a specific reason for using them. A coach must remember that he gets what he emphasizes. The coach should tell players what to do, show them what to do, and make sure they do it the right way. That is the essence of coaching. Everything that players do on the field is a reflection of their coaching. The good and the bad come back to the coach. The coach is either coaching the players to do it or is allowing them to do it. Lou Holtz said, "Perfection is possible if you accept nothing less."

•   **Skill and technique work** (10 minutes): For the receivers and quarterbacks, this period refers to individual routes on air. Typically, the receivers split up into three separate lines: left side, right side, and slots. We start with the shorter routes (e.g., the three-step stuff in the quick game) and work our way up to the intermediate passes, then to the deeper vertical down-the-field throws. Players work on the location and timing for each specific route. The split and depth of the route are cleaned up, and both quarterbacks and receivers get on the same page.

•   **Combination and group work, one-on-ones** (10 to 15 minutes): Group work can include several different drills versus defensive players. During one-on-ones, a receiver and quarterback work routes versus a defensive back playing man to man. This is a great period for receivers to work on releases, hands, and separation skills versus both off and press coverage. This drill should be done out in the field, and at some point during the week, it should also be moved down in the red zone. Other group drills will be discussed in detail in later chapters.

- **Seven-on-seven drills** (15 to 20 minutes): The seven-on-seven, or skeleton, drill is when the offense works specifically on the drop-back passing game. Most play-action, sprint-out, and bootleg plays should be run in the team (11-on-11) period. The seven-on-seven drill consists of the five eligible receivers and the quarterback and center versus the four defensive backs and three linebackers who are working their various coverage drops. This period should be modified over the course of the practice week to include various situations such as third downs, red zone, and tight-zone passing.

- **11-on-11, or team, situational by day** (50 to 60 minutes): The 11-on-11 practice drills should be situational and can be split up into different segments of practice (typically in 10-, 15-, or 20-minute blocks). They can also be split up by number of plays, depending on how the head coach wants the period to be organized. The key is to feature a lot of different situations in different areas of practice. For example, this segment of practice should include a set of plays for first and 10, a set of plays for third down, and a set of plays for red zone and tight zone. We emphasize different situations on different days so the players are familiar with what type of plays to expect in the various areas of the field.

Situations to Practice in Team Periods

First and 10 yards

Second and medium

Second and long

Third and 2 or 3 yards

Third and 4 to 6 yards

Third and 7 to 10 yards

Third and 10-plus yards

Red-zone fringe: +35-yard line to the +20-yard line

Red zone: +20-yard line to the 12-yard line

Tight zone: +12-yard line to the goal line

Two-point plays from the +3-yard line

Short yardage: third and 1 yard

Goal line: inside the +5-yard line

Backed up inside own 3-yard line coming out

Two-minute drill at the end of the first half

Two-minute drill at the end of the game

Last three plays of the game or Hail Mary to win the game when behind

Four-minute drill when running out the clock and the offense is ahead

The Situations to Practice in Team Periods sidebar lists just a few situations that come up over the course of a game. Players must understand that each of these situations is unique and that they will get specific looks from the defense in each situation. They must also know that they need to learn certain things offensively for each situation. When these things are practiced by situation, it allows the coaches to use the time in practice as a teachable moment and to emphasize how they want the team to respond in each specific situation. Remember, coaches get what they emphasize!

Summary

To me, practice is everything. Energy and enthusiasm are a part of a great practice environment. You can't be great at anything without a passion for what you are doing. If this is not a part of the practice environment, then you are missing the straw that mixes the drink. Practice is the game in many ways, because if you can execute the plan in practice at a high level over and over, your chances of getting what you want on game day greatly improve. Repetition, repetition, repetition. William Hazlitt was right when he said that we need to cease thinking about something in order to do it right. The repetition makes the skill exceptional. That's the beauty of practice. This leads us into our next set of specific skills, which are those related to ball security. These are the skills that often separate winning and losing.

3

Ball Security

As a kid, I loved to watch NFL playoff games with my father. One game that left a real impact on me was the 1988 AFC championship game between the visiting Cleveland Browns and the Denver Broncos. It was a cold wintry day in Denver. The winner of the game would advance to the Super Bowl. The Broncos were led by the great John Elway, the Browns by cerebral hometown boy Bernie Kosar at quarterback. The Browns also had a bruising running back named Earnest Byner. The Browns were down 21-3 midway through the game, but in the second half, the Browns roared back thanks to Kosar's leadership and Byner's playmaking out of the backfield. With 1:12 left in the game, the Browns were on the 9-yard line, ready to score and tie the game. Byner broke through a huge hole on the left side of the Broncos' line on a draw play. It looked like a sure touchdown. As Byner got to the 3-yard line, Broncos defensive back Jeremiah Castille came out of nowhere. Castille tried to strip the ball. Byner was hit from the side, the ball popped out, and the Broncos recovered it on their own 2-yard line. The Broncos took an intentional safety and won the game 38 to 33.

It was so painful to watch the emotional roller coaster that Byner was riding. One moment he was on the verge of scoring the winning touchdown to send his team to the Super Bowl; the next he made the critical mistake that changed the team's fortune, and they lost the game. It was heartbreaking to watch Byner kneel on the sidelines alone with his head down, knowing that had he just held onto the ball Cleveland would have advanced to the Super Bowl. "What Earnest didn't see is what created the problem for us," said Marty Schottenheimer, the Browns head coach. "Earnest never saw him coming." In the last chapter, we talked about discipline and the pain of regret. Earnest Byner has had to live with his painful mistake for a long time.

Earnest Byner was a tremendous player, and Cleveland would have never been in the AFC championship game without him. He took a lot of heat from Browns fans, but many overlooked the fact that Byner was superb up to that point. He had rushed for 67 yards and had seven receptions for 120 yards and two touchdowns. Byner was a fine player. He was traded a year later and ended up winning a Super Bowl with the Washington Redskins, but he carries the pain of that fumble to this day. It's a great reminder to always be aware of ball security. There may be a guy you don't see.

Respect the Football

Almost as long as I have been playing and coaching the game, at both the college and pro levels, coaches have harped on the importance of ball security. Ball security is easily the most important factor in winning and losing games. In football, the team that protects the ball the best often wins the game. In 2008, the Oklahoma Sooners and the Florida Gators had the fewest turnovers in the United States. It wasn't a surprise that the two teams that took care of the ball the best ended up in the national championship that season. Jim Mora Sr., long-time NFL head coach, used to preach the value of protecting the ball when I worked for him in the late 1990s with the Indianapolis Colts. Ever since then, the first thing I emphasize every week of the season is ball security.

I spent two seasons with Jerry Rice, who scored 208 touchdowns as a player, more than any other player in the history of the game. It is one of the iconic records in all sports. But the thing about Jerry was that he was such a fundamentally sound player in every respect. And he took immense pride in his ball security. He carried the ball high and tight, and when he got into the open field, he always pinned the ball on his shoulder pads to protect it from the man he couldn't see. He said it's always the guy you can't see who can pop the ball loose. Jerry set a great example for all players—the greatest scorer of all time took the most pride in his ball security and, more important, in how he carried the ball.

In college football, you can see the trend of the finest teams in the country and how their ability to protect the football translates to winning on the field. Between 2007 and 2011, the top five teams in turnover ratio in college football were typically +15 or better, with the best team between +20 and +23. (See table 3.1 for some examples.) That means the teams get about 30 takeaways (or more) on defense, and on offense, they are in the low teens in turnovers. Thus, the defense is averaging about 3 turnovers a game, and the offense is giving up 1 or fewer a game.

Ball Security Is Job Security

For NFL players and coaches alike, ball security is definitely job security. The players who don't secure the ball aren't around long. The teams that don't secure the ball find new coaches. As good as the college numbers were for the teams shown in table 3.1, they pale when compared to the New England

TABLE 3.1   NCAA Leaders in Turnover Margin, 2007 to 2011

Year	School	Turnovers gained	Turnovers lost	Margin	Wins	Losses
2007	LSU*	36	16	+20	12	2
2007	Kansas	35	14	+21	12	1
2008	Florida*	35	13	+22	13	1
2008	Oklahoma	34	11	+23	12	2
2009	Alabama*	31	12	+19	14	0
2009	Rutgers	34	14	+20	9	4
2009	Air Force	34	12	+22	8	5
2010	Auburn*	22	17	+5	14	0
2010	Tulsa	36	19	+17	10	3
2010	Virginia Tech	32	13	+19	11	3
2011	Oklahoma State	44	23	+21	12	1
2011	LSU	30	10	+20	13	1

*National champion

Patriots in the 2010 season. In 2010, the Patriots set an NFL record with 10 turnovers lost in a 16-game regular season. That is far fewer than 1 turnover a game. In fact, the Patriots set an NFL record of six straight games without a single turnover. They went 14-2 in the regular season, and although they didn't go on to win the Super Bowl, they had by far the best NFL season in the history of the game for offensive ball security. They ended up a whopping +28 in turnover margin. Here are some other impressive numbers: The team had 507 passes in 2010 and threw only five interceptions. Along with that, they had only five fumbles in the 16-game season, giving them an NFL record low of a total of 10 turnovers for the 16-game season. The previous record had been set by the Miami Dolphins at 13.

Bill Parcells preached taking care of the ball as much as anyone. In a 2010 *Boston Globe* article, Parcells said this about not turning the ball over: "This is going to sound kind of funny, but at the very worst it means you're able to punt the ball and keep field position. I'm serious. That may not sound like much, but it is. Of course, at best, when you're not turning it over it means you're scoring and not giving them opportunities." In football, sometimes it's not a bad thing to punt the ball, as long as you are taking care of it and not turning it over to the other team on a short field. If you can punt and play good defense, you have a chance to win every game. Many coaches have made a career out of this strategy. Just don't give the ball away; that is what kills a team. It gives the opponent a short field, and they don't have to go very far to score. That's why the correlation between winning and not turning the ball over is so high. Winning teams and great coaches and players take great pride in this area of the game.

Four Points of Pressure

Securing the ball properly starts with four points of pressure. First, the palm of the hand must wrap around and secure the point of the football (figure 3.1). Next, the forearm applies pressure on the pigskin (figure 3.2) to pin it tightly against the body so there is no air between the ball and the body; the player must also ensure that the ball isn't exposed so the defender can take a shot at the leather. The next point of pressure is the biceps. The forearm and biceps put pressure on the ball like a vise and secure it to the body (figure 3.3). The last point is the rib cage (figure 3.4a) or the upper shoulder pad (figure 3.4b) if the ball is held higher.

FIGURE 3.1 Four points of pressure: Palm wraps around the point of the ball.

FIGURE 3.2 Four points of pressure: Forearm pins the ball to the body.

FIGURE 3.3 Four points of pressure: Biceps pressures the ball like a vise.

FIGURE 3.4 Four points of pressure: Ball is pinned against *(a)* the rib cage or *(b)* the upper shoulder pad.

Now the ball is protected by these four points of pressure in what we call a *locked position*. The forearm must cover the fat part of the ball so that there is as little leather exposed as possible. Players with small hands and forearms may have a difficult time wrapping the football and covering up the leather. These players must do a great job of covering up with two hands in traffic (figure 3.5).

Short players who have small hands and short arms sometimes have a problem getting a good fit. Because of their short arms, they expose too much leather on the football, and the ball can be vulnerable because of this. These players have to work hard to maintain a good fit, and they must learn to get two hands on the ball in traffic. They must focus on protecting the ball early in their careers, because if a player gets the reputation of a small guy who has a fumbling problem, it's difficult to shake that reputation.

FIGURE 3.5 Securing the ball with both hands.

Handling Defensive Pressure

Don't fight pressure. One of the most difficult ball security skills to learn is to keep the fit when the defender starts to pull at the ball. A good defensive player will put his hand on the tip of the ball and try to pry the ball out of the receiver's hands (figure 3.6*a*). The natural reaction is to pull against this pressure, but this is the wrong thing to do because it works against the tight fit that the receiver has on the ball. When the defensive player pulls to pry open the vise, the receiver should keep the ball locked up and relax his upper body to twist and turn with the force of the defender (figure 3.6*b*). The offensive player actually lets the defender spin him like a top but never allows any breaks in the four points of pressure. The player gets spun around, but the ball stays locked up.

FIGURE 3.6   Defensive pressure: *(a)* Defender puts his hand on the tip of the ball to try to pry it out of the receiver's hands; *(b)* the receiver keeps the ball locked up and turns with the force of the defender.

Running After the Catch

When a player is running with the ball, we should see no air in the ball (figure 3.7). Receivers, especially young receivers, get excited when they get the ball in open space. The first thing they want to do is run as fast as they can and make somebody miss. The natural thing to do when you want to run fast is to get loose and careless with the ball. In practice, coaches call out, "Too much air in the ball!" That means the ball is too far away from the body. We developed a rule that whenever a receiver is shown on TV or in a picture while carrying the ball in his hands, the ball better be tight to the body. When we see a receiver in a picture and the ball is out from his body, we sure let him know. Most of the time, we see pictures of our guys with the ball locked up. We are proud of the four points of pressure.

Securing the Ball in Traffic

You must learn to keep two hands on the ball in traffic (figure 3.8). When you get in traffic with two or more defenders converging on you, you need to wrap up the ball with two hands (see figure 3.5) and protect it at all costs. This is playing smart. When there are multiple defenders going after the ball, you want to expose the ball as little as possible. Do the smart thing and protect it in traffic.

FIGURE 3.7 When a receiver is running in open space, we should see no air in the ball. The receiver must keep the ball close to the body.

FIGURE 3.8 In traffic, a receiver must keep both hands on the ball.

Ball Security Drills

Ball security drills are the first thing that we emphasize in practice on Monday of each week. Because ball security is so critical to winning football games, it always receives the highest priority in our drill progression. Ball security drills are the first thing we focus on for the week.

Partner Chop, Chop, Pull

SETUP: Two players, one on offense and one on defense, prepare to execute the drill from the sideline to the hash mark.

EXECUTION:

1. To start the drill, the coach throws the ball to the offensive player. The offensive player secures the ball in his right hand—using four points of pressure—and strides toward the hash mark. The offensive player is moving at a slow jog. The emphasis is on the technique of securing the football.

2. The defensive player punches and clubs at the ball, trying to dislodge it. The defensive player takes a full club at the ball over the top (figure 3.9a) and underneath (figure 3.9b) a couple times to make sure it is secured properly.

3. After clubbing and swatting at the ball a couple times, the defender tries to grab at the point of the ball and pull (figure 3.9c). On this pull, the offensive player keeps the ball high and tight in a locked position and allows the defensive player to spin him all the way around.

4. After reaching the hash mark, the offensive player switches the ball to his left hand and returns to the sideline as the defensive player again tries to strip the ball.

COACHING POINTS: The defensive intensity makes the drill realistic, so the defender must not take it easy on the offensive player. When the defender pulls on the point of the ball, the force should spin the offensive player completely around.

FIGURE 3.9 Partner chop, chop, pull: *(a)* Defensive player clubs the ball on the top; *(b)* defensive player clubs the ball underneath; *(c)* defensive player grabs the point of the ball and pulls.

Distraction Tunnel Drill

SETUP: Five or six players get in position for the drill. Four to six players line up on each side of a single player to form a tunnel. The single player inside the tunnel stands just inside the first two players (figure 3.10). The coach stands at the front of the tunnel with a football.

EXECUTION:

1. The coach throws the football to the player inside the tunnel.
2. The first two players in line move their hands back and forth to try to distract the receiver catching the ball.
3. The receiver catches the ball and then turns inside the human tunnel and runs through it.
4. The players on either side of the tunnel punch, slap, and pull at the ball to try to get it out as the receiver runs through the tunnel.
5. Each player rotates through until all the players have had a chance to run through the tunnel.

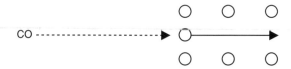

FIGURE 3.10 Distraction tunnel drill.

COACHING POINTS:

- The first two players in the tunnel are in front of the receiver to distract him from catching the ball. When players rotate, they need to realign with this in mind.
- After catching the ball, the receiver moves through the tunnel swiftly.
- The tunnel players reach for and grab at the ball, but they should not impede the receiver's progress too much. They should allow the receiver to keep moving through the tunnel.

Run Around Right Hand, Left Hand

SETUP: Receivers line up single file on a yard line. A coach with a football stands to one side.

EXECUTION:

1. The coach throws the ball to the first receiver in line.
2. The receiver runs 5 yards, puts his right hand on the ground, and runs a circle around it while securing the ball high and tight with his left hand (figure 3.11*a*).
3. The receiver runs another 5 yards, touches his left hand to the ground, and runs around his left hand while securing the ball in his right hand (figure 3.11*b*).

FIGURE 3.11   Run around right hand, left hand drill: *(a)* Receiver puts right hand on ground and circles; *(b)* receiver puts left hand on ground and circles.

Fireman's Roll

The fireman's roll is a penalty drill that I learned from a good friend of mine named Kirby Wilson. Kirby is a fine NFL assistant who has won two Super Bowls with Tampa and Pittsburgh. I got this drill from Kirby when he was the running backs coach at Iowa State University. Kirby had a rule that if any running back fumbled the football in a game or practice, the whole group had to do fireman's rolls as punishment. A fireman's roll is exactly what it sounds like. Every player has a ball locked up in four points of pressure. The player lies down and rolls as if he were on fire and trying to put out the flames, keeping the ball tight to his body. Rolling across the field and back is a mighty punishment that players won't soon forget.

SETUP: Players start on the sideline. Each player has a ball.

EXECUTION:

- Each player locks the ball high and tight in four points of pressure.
- Players lie down and roll (figure 3.12) the entire width of the field, from sideline to sideline.
- Down and back is a good place to start. I guarantee it will make an impression on the players.
- If fumbles continue, the coach can add more trips as a deterrent.

COACHING POINTS:

- As the players roll, they must keep the ball in a good fit, tight on their body.
- Players must roll in a straight line.
- This is a punishment drill that players will remember. It directly shows them the pain that turnovers will inflict on the team. It is a reminder that turnovers lose games. Players must never forget that.

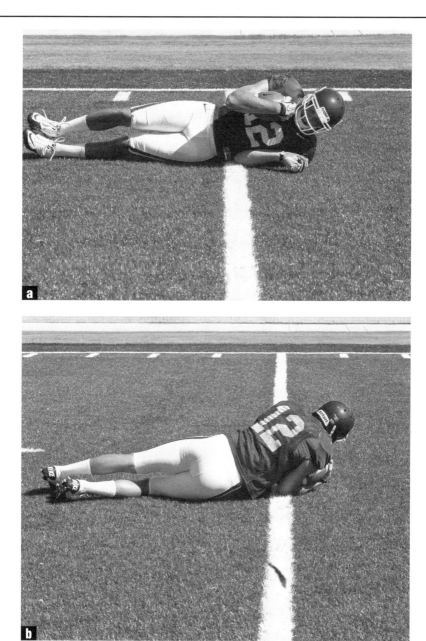

FIGURE 3.12 Fireman's roll: With the ball locked high and tight in four points of pressure, *(a)* the player lies on the field and *(b)* rolls to the sideline.

Summary

Coaches get what they emphasize. Ball security is an area of the game in which there can be no compromise. It is always the first thing I emphasize, and it must be consistently reinforced. Ball security is always the first thing I talk about at the beginning of training camp, and I never assume that it is understood. Until young players have been in really tough game situations, I always give them extra work on ball security after practice to help get them ready. In the National Football League, where players come and go, we had a saying: "Good players don't fumble." It really is true. Good players learn the importance of taking care of the football, and then they take tremendous pride in the way they handle it. To see Jerry Rice secure the ball in the open field was a thing of beauty. A great ballcarrier sends a message to the world by the way he locks up the football. Make it part of your fiber as a player so it becomes who you are. In the end, it hits to the core of your pride as a ballcarrier. You can see it in how the great ones carry the football.

4

Stance

Al Pacino, one of the great American actors of our time, played the part of a professional head football coach in the movie *Any Given Sunday*. At the peak of the movie, Al Pacino's character, a battered old coach who is riding a losing streak and is fighting for his team and his job, draws his team in and begins making the parallel between football and life. In this scene, the filmmakers captured the essence of a team in crisis. Pacino's character explains to his team that football, like life, is a game of inches. One step too quick or too late and you don't quite get there; one step too slow or too fast and you don't quite catch the ball. He pressed his team to fight for that inch because all those inches would make the difference between winning and losing.

This chapter is about fighting for inches, and in particular, fighting for that very first inch.

Timing is critical in football, particularly in the passing game. In professional football, the pass rush is so incredibly fast and effective. NFL defensive linemen are some of the greatest athletes in the world. They are big, fast, and nasty. They get paid an enormous amount of money to get to the quarterback, and they spend 12 months of the year training to meet that goal.

Pass protection is crucial to the offense's ability to execute the passing game. A coach can draw up all the fancy passes he wants, but if these plays aren't protected, the quarterback won't get the passes off. The average fan thinks that pass protection is the job of the offensive line. In the NFL, you learn quickly that pass protection is everybody's responsibility. Offensive linemen must move their feet to stay in front of their men and keep them away from the quarterback. Running backs must get their pads down, square up, and effectively pick up the blitzing linebacker. The quarterback must get away from center smoothly and efficiently, clearly and accurately read the defense, and deliver the ball quickly and precisely before the rush hits him.

The receiver also has an important job in pass protection. The receiver is fighting the clock. His job is to evaluate the defense, explode off the football with the proper release, get up the field, execute his route at the proper depth, and get open at the proper time. Proper depth and reception area are critical to the receiver's job.

Players at every position are fighting the timing element the instant the ball is snapped and put into play. All 22 players on the field are poised to explode into action when that ball is snapped. The players who get off cleanly and efficiently will gain the edge on every specific play. On average, 150 offensive and defensive plays are run in every game. On each of these plays, every player is poised for that split second when the ball is snapped, and every player tries to get that split-second advantage to get the upper hand on his opponent. This explosion off the ball is when the one-on-one battle begins. It is very similar to a fighter who can use his quick hands to land a jab before his opponent reacts. That quickness is the advantage he needs to beat the defender to the punch. It's the same thing on a football field: The man who gets to the spot first gains the advantage.

Two-Point Stance

Every athletic movement in sports starts with the proper body position and the proper stance. A common thread in all sports is that the body has to bend to be put in motion. The legs, hips, waist, arms, and neck all have to move in position to put the body in motion. The proper stance is the foundation for any athletic movement. When I was a kid, the stance was the first thing my coaches talked about. They called it the breakdown position. The breakdown position is the universal athletic position in which the feet are staggered, the weight is on the balls of the feet, and the shoulders are over the toes (figure 4.1). The player is in a good bent athletic posture.

Nothing is more frustrating than seeing a player in a poor stance. If the player is wrong from the start, he will have difficulty doing anything else right once the ball is snapped. This chapter is about the split second before the ball is snapped and the position that the receiver's body needs to be in so he can do his job at maximum efficiency.

Our receivers use a two-point stance (figure 4.2). This gives the player the best opportunity to come off the ball at full speed and release off any secondary technique he sees. It also allows the player to get a presnap read on the coverage so he can anticipate and get in to his conversion quicker.

At one time, receivers used a three-point stance. You can see this in old highlight films. When the passing game became more sophisticated, the defenses started using more coverages, and the routes began to have more conversions.

In today's game, the two-point stance is more effective than the three-point stance. The two-point stance makes it so much easier for the player

FIGURE 4.1 Breakdown athletic position: feet staggered, weight on balls of feet, shoulders over toes. *(a)* Front view; *(b)* side view.

to see the defense so he can make the proper adjustments. However, one problem with the two-point stance is that some players have a tendency to relax and stand tall, getting in a poor position before the ball is snapped. If the receiver is relaxed and standing tall in the two-point stance, when the ball is snapped, he must drop his hips so he can explode off the line of scrimmage. An activated stance, on the other hand, means the receiver is already coiled up; therefore, when the ball is snapped, the receiver gets off on the snap, not after the snap.

FIGURE 4.2 Two-point stance.

Hand and Arm Placement

The arms should be bent with the elbows in at the sides (figure 4.3). The hands should be relaxed and open. Some young players are taught to place their fists together and stick their elbows out. My experience tells me that this is not the proper position for the hands. You want quickness, speed, and explosion. The body moves faster and reacts quicker from a loose position. The best example of this is a boxer. Boxers who are tight, rigid, and robotic are slow. Boxers who are loose and fluid are quick and responsive. That's why you want the hands open. When you make a fist, your upper body tenses, and it slows you down. In your stance, you should relax and open your hands so you will move quicker.

FIGURE 4.3 Hand and arm position in the stance.

Activate

Many coaches use buzzwords for techniques that they want players to remember and apply quickly in the heat of the moment. *Activate* is a buzzword that I use to remind players about the proper stance. Activate refers to the ready position that the body is in just before it uncoils to run fast. A great example of this is the position that sprinters get in at the beginning of the 100-meter dash at the Olympics. It is a tense crouching position (figure 4.4). In track, sprinters are in this position the split second before the gun goes off at the beginning of the race. It's the position that the body is in the split second before "get set" and the crack of the gun. That's what it means to get in an activated position.

> **"If you want to get open, you have to run as fast as you can!"**
>
> *Tom Moore, former NFL offensive coordinator for the Indianapolis Colts*

Animals use this position all the time. Think of the split second when the cheetah sinks her hips and drops her upper body right before she explodes down the plains to run down her prey. I used to have a Labrador retriever

FIGURE 4.4   Activate position, crouched and ready.

that was trained to retrieve. When the dog was sitting, he couldn't leave until he was given the command. When the dummy was thrown out, the dog wanted to go for it so bad, but he would just stay crouched and ready to explode until the OK was given.

An activated position is not supposed to be comfortable or relaxed. In this position, the player is like a tense uncoiled spring that is ready to be unleashed on the world. That's the best explanation of how the presnap body position should feel.

Evaluating the Defensive Technique

In this section, we'll look at two specific techniques: off coverage and press coverage. Recognizing these two techniques is critical because the receiver will need to make some slight adjustments in his stance and alignment based on whether he is getting press or off technique from the defender.

In off coverage, the defender is playing 6 or 7 yards off the line of scrimmage in a position where the receiver can run off the ball without any obstruction from the defense. Typically, off technique is played with Cover 3 (a three-deep zone defense), Quarter Cover 4 (a four-deep defense), or Off Cover 1 (a man-free defense) (figure 4.5). Cover 3 features three deep secondary players, and Cover 4 has four secondary players, each covering a deep quarter of the field. Figure 4.5*c* shows Cover 1 with off coverage by the corners. Cover 1 is man-to-man coverage by the five underneath players. The free safety plays deep down the middle and protects against the

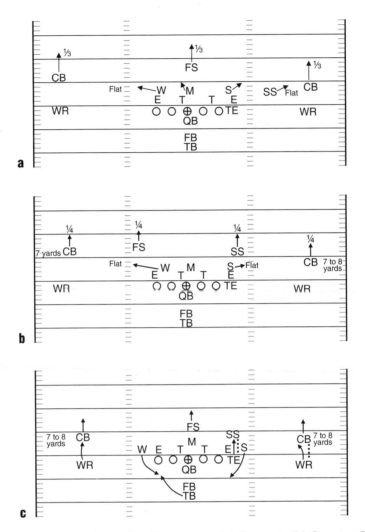

FIGURE 4.5 Defenses played in off coverage: *(a)* Cover 3; *(b)* Quarter Cover 4; *(c)* Off Cover 1.

deep pass. The corners will probably play inside technique and alignment on each wide receiver.

To understand the need for a great stance, you also need to recognize press coverage. Press coverage is just as the name suggests. The defender walks right up to the line of scrimmage and is looking to bump and run the receiver. Figure 4.6 shows Cover 1 press coverage. In Cover 1, five defenders play man coverage. One deep safety protects against deep balls down the middle of the field. The corners are up on the line of scrimmage in an inside alignment.

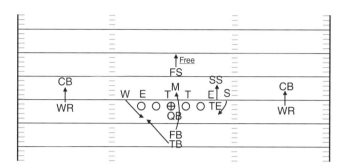

FIGURE 4.6 Press coverage.

Release

Receivers need to get off on the snap. The cadence should be an advantage for the offensive football team. The offense knows when the ball is going to be snapped; the defense doesn't. The offense must use that cadence to its advantage. Sometimes the offense will go on the first sound the quarterback makes, and sometimes the offense will go on a two count to throw the defense off rhythm. Other times the offense might use a freeze count or hard count and not snap the football at all, trying to get the defense to jump offside. Every offensive player must learn to get off on the snap. When we watch film, I want to see the snap of the football and the receiver moving almost simultaneously. There shouldn't be a delay between when the ball is snapped and when the receiver comes off the ball (figure 4.7). We call those

FIGURE 4.7 The receiver comes off the ball when the ball is snapped.

late offs. We want the whole offense roaring down on the defense together as one unit when the ball is snapped.

As a receiver, you must make sure that you can see the ball out of the corner of your vision. For a receiver in an upright position, there is never an excuse to jump off the ball. These types of penalties are inexcusable. At the college or professional levels, it is often difficult for the receiver to hear the snap count because the receiver's alignment has him so far removed from the quarterback. That is why the receiver must be prepared to see the ball snapped. As an offensive unit, we want no late offs at any position.

When you release on the snap, you should then run to get open. Every route that a receiver runs begins with the takeoff, the nine routes, or the go ball! A nine route is a vertical deep route, which is run straight down the field. We teach route running at one speed—full speed. Tom Moore was my offensive coordinator when I coached receivers for the Indianapolis Colts. He was a veteran NFL coach who had been with several teams. He started out in pro ball coaching with the Pittsburgh Steelers in the 1970s. He coached two hall of fame receivers named Lynn Swann and John Stallworth. He had a philosophy on route running that has become my philosophy to this day. His philosophy was simply that if you want to get open, you have to run as hard as you can. The best way to get open is to spring off the football and make the defender think you are going to run a go ball every play. To get open, a receiver has to put the defender in a vulnerable position by getting the defender's hips open and getting him running vertically. By getting the defender to open up and play the deep ball, the receiver is free to break off his route short and create the separation he needs to get open. The key is that it doesn't matter how fast you are. You just have to come off the ball at full speed and get into a dead run as fast as possible. To be able to do that, you have to be in a great stance!

I love watching animal shows on television. The struggle for survival in the wild involves real drama. These stories of real life can be related to our challenges in sports. I came across a piece that I found on YouTube. It was a short clip about a cheetah and her hunt of a mule deer on the plains of Africa. The footage blew me away. The way she identified her prey, zeroed in on it, and initiated the hunt was amazing. What really blew me away was the moment of truth when she crouched down and the hairs on her back started to stand up. She went from a dead stop to 60 miles per hour in about 3 seconds! Wow, absolutely amazing! That's how I want our receivers to come off the ball—0 to 60 in a matter of about 6 or 7 yards. I couldn't wait to show this clip to my guys. The visual is worth a thousand words. That cheetah blew the doors off! "Let the cheetahs out" became my battle cry on the practice field. You have to get out and run!

Releasing Against an Off Technique Defender

Stand with your feet staggered, a little wider than shoulder-width apart. The feet should be staggered with the front foot on the line of scrimmage. To practice getting into this position, start in a sprinter's stance with both hands on the ground as if you were in the blocks for a track event, one foot staggered in front of the other (figure 4.8*a*). Now stand up (figure 4.8*b*). This is how your feet should be staggered. If you stand straight up, stagger your feet, and then drop your back knee to the heel of your front foot, the position where your back foot hits the ground is where you should stagger the back foot.

Use a narrow base like that of a sprinter in the starting blocks. A narrow base means that the space between the feet is narrow, only 4 to 5 inches. A receiver's stance is designed for speed, unlike a lineman's stance, which is wide and built for power. A receiver must transfer from a standing start to a full sprint as quickly as possible. A narrow base will help the receiver get to top speed faster.

Stand with your legs bent and ready to uncoil (figure 4.9). Think of a dog in a crouch position a split second before he fetches a bone. The legs are bent and flexed. That is the position the receiver should be in before the snap of the ball. The player shouldn't be relaxed and straight legged. He should be poised and ready to go.

Shift your weight to the balls of your feet. The weight should be on the balls of the feet so that weight can be transferred through the legs into a vertical sprint. The strong leg muscles can only generate power and speed if the weight is transferred by first having weight on the balls of the feet.

FIGURE 4.8   Practice staggering the feet: *(a)* getting into a sprinter's stance with both hands on the ground; *(b)* standing up.

FIGURE 4.9 Legs are bent and ready to uncoil.

Stand with the shoulder pads low. A receiver needs to have low shoulder pads and high hands (figure 4.10). I use the phrase "high hands, low pads." This body position gives the defense the least amount of body surface to use to hold up the receiver. Offensive players should use this simple rule—the smaller the body surface available for the defense to hold up, the more difficult it is for the defense to hit the offensive player.

FIGURE 4.10 High hands, low pads.

Lean your upper body over the front foot. By leaning forward, you ensure that your body weight is over your front foot so you can explode and sprint forward. In addition, this will again limit the body surface for the defender to hit.

Hold your hands chest high. The hands should be held chest high with the fingers slightly curled. Don't keep the hands balled into a fist. Keep the palms open and the hands ready to be active so you can use them to get off the line of scrimmage.

Place 80 percent of your weight on your front foot (your feet are staggered). Versus off coverage, you want all of your momentum on the snap to be heading straight off the ball as fast as possible. You need to get the majority of your weight on the front foot so you can explode vertically upfield. The key versus an off technique is that you need to release straight up the field as fast as you can with no false steps. With no defender in your way, all your concentration can be on exploding off the ball vertically at full speed.

When releasing versus off coverage, you must learn to come off the ball without any false steps (figure 4.11). You want to roll off the front foot. The first step should be the back foot heading straight up the field. Some players have a bad habit of picking up the front foot and putting it down. This is a false step. The ball has been snapped, but the receiver isn't going anywhere. He is wasting time.

Your eyes must see the ball to see the snap. In a loud environment, a receiver will not be able to hear the snap count. Versus an off technique, the receiver should see the snap in his peripheral vision. Versus press coverage, the receiver's attention will sometimes have to turn toward the defender.

FIGURE 4.11 First step on release: *(a)* roll off the front foot; *(b)* first step is with the back foot straight upfield.

This can be difficult in a loud environment. At times, the receiver will have to use a combination of an audible snap count and his peripheral vision to get the best possible jump on the snap.

On the snap, you need to eat up the defensive back's cushion (figure 4.12). Eating up his cushion means cutting down the distance between you and the defender as quickly as possible. The quicker you can eat up his cushion, the faster you can get him out of his comfort zone. You will get open quicker and more effectively. The quicker and more consistently you get open, the more balls you will catch. It is really that simple. It all starts with how you get off on the snap.

FIGURE 4.12 *(a)* The receiver eats up the defensive back's cushion *(b)* by reducing the distance between the defensive back and the receiver as quickly as possible.

Releasing Against a Press Defender

Against a press defender, you have to make a few adjustments. Against press coverage, you may need to work laterally, so you want your body position to allow lateral movement. Instead of putting most of your weight on your front foot, you should distribute your weight 50–50 on both feet and straighten up a little (figure 4.13).

Versus press coverage or bump man to man, you want to make an adjustment in your stance. The situation has now changed. You don't want to run straight off the ball because you have a defender in front of you. If you run straight into him, your route will be totally disrupted, and you will take way too long to get to the depth of your route. You would be playing right into the hands of the defense. Therefore, you should balance your stance with your weight evenly distributed between both feet. This will allow you to work laterally, side to side, to avoid the defender on the line of scrimmage and get up the field vertically to the proper depth while maintaining the integrity and timing of the pattern.

A receiver never wants to get into a pushing contest with the defensive back. Defenders are taught to get their hands on the receiver at the line of scrimmage to slow him down. My experience is that if the defender can't hold you and slow you down, he can't cover you. So the best thing the receiver can do is make the guy miss by working laterally and then up the field as fast as possible.

FIGURE 4.13 Against a press defender, the receiver stands a little straighter and balances his weight on both feet.

Versus press coverage, you want low pads and high hands. When releasing off press coverage, you need to limit the body surface available for the defender to get his hands on. The defender will try to slow you down by putting his hands on you and trying to get to your chest and shoulder pads. As a receiver, you must limit your body surface as much as possible. In this situation, you want your hands chest high and your shoulder pads down (figure 4.14). The player who gets hands on the other first gains control of the situation. That's why the wide out must have high hands in the presnap. With your hands high in the presnap, you are already there before the ball is put in play. The defender can't beat you to the mark. This is an age-old battle of hand-to-hand combat that will determine who wins on the most critical passing downs of the game.

FIGURE 4.14 Against a press defender, the receiver's hands are chest high, and his shoulder pads are down.

Get-Off Drill

SETUP: Two coaches kneel about 10 yards apart from each other on a yard line. The coaches will use a ball on a stick to indicate the center snap. Two players at a time execute the drill.

EXECUTION:

1. The players get in position on the line of scrimmage.
2. Coach 1 uses a cadence and moves the ball on the snap or movement of the stick.
3. The players move on the cadence and ball movement. They explode off the ball hard with no false steps and run to the next line of scrimmage, where coach 2 is waiting (figure 4.15).
4. The players line up again on the next line of scrimmage, similar to a no-huddle offense. The receivers have to get set, listen to coach 2's cadence, and get off on the snap again.
5. Coach 2 simulates another snap count. The players get off on the cadence and ball movement. In all, the drill should cover about 20 yards.

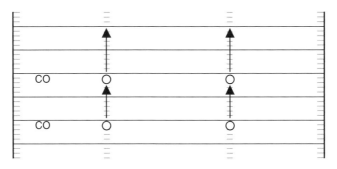

FIGURE 4.15   Get-off drill.

COACHING POINTS: Players should concentrate on getting in a good stance and exploding off on the snap cleanly with no false steps.

Summary

The stance is the fundamental building block of great receiver play. It is one of the most overlooked and underemphasized areas of football. The stance is truly the foundation on which the rest of the receiver's fundamentals are built. The longer I am around the game of football and witness great coaches, the more I see that great coaches emphasize stance and get-off, regardless of a player's position. It is amazing to see; all you have to do is turn on the film. Whether that player is an offensive lineman or a defensive tackle, the initial stance and get-off are the first fundamentals that allow the player to play with sound and strong skill. As a coach, I have come to love seeing a player in the best position to play before the ball is snapped. It is a sense of pride to me, and it is a huge reminder that the mastery of the little things is what makes the difference in being a champion.

5
Catching

Catching the football is a challenging skill. And it becomes even more challenging when a receiver must catch the ball while changing directions and running full speed through traffic between players who are trained to hit him. Doing it well takes great focus, concentration, sound fundamentals, and great confidence, which come directly from repetition and experience.

Catching the football is the skill that defines the position of wide receiver. It is what receivers are put into the game to do: get open, make plays, and catch the ball when it is thrown to them. An important factor is where the receiver places his hands and his eyes. Tracking the flight of the football is also important. A lot of variables come into play in games when receivers execute full-speed cuts and must get their hands and body in position to make plays on the ball as defenders are doing everything in their power to stop the completion from happening. It takes incredible skill and a special intensity of focus to do this at a high level. Receivers must also have a fundamental understanding of the physics of moving objects as well as how the schematic pieces of offenses and defenses are put together.

Catching the ball is a skill. Like any skill, a series of movements must come into play in order to have a successful outcome. It's not always easy to put so many moving parts into words. Athletes sometimes take something that seems so difficult and make it look effortless and smooth. That surely applies in the case of catching the football. Those players who can do it well have a higher ability to focus—they have the ability to slow down very complex sets of movements in their mind and compartmentalize those movements almost in slow motion. It's like the scene in the movie *The Matrix* when the lead actor is leaning back and the bullets are going by him in slow motion. Players with great ball skills are able to slow down very fast movements and react as if they were in slow motion. These are players with superior eye–hand skills or movements. They tend to be very quick and accurate, and they are very sure of themselves, especially their hands. Like an old gunfighter, a boxer, or a karate man, the great receivers have quick, sure hands.

The ability to catch the ball with soft, sure hands is the defining skill of the position. Catching a football in the air is a skill that takes a combination of vision, upper-body positioning, hand placement, eye–hand coordination, and a soft touch.

Vision

Receivers must be able to catch all kinds of passes from a variety of positions all over the field, from dart passes from 5 or 6 yards away, to intermediate passes from 12 to 15 yards away, to deeper throws on an arc 40 to 50 yards down the field. Then there is the bullet pass in the red zone that is thrown on a line through all kinds of arms and pads. To catch all of these passes, a receiver must have good vision. Coaches can evaluate players' vision by throwing a lot of different balls to them.

This really hit home with me in 1998 when I was coaching with the Indianapolis Colts. Three or four days a week during off-season training, we were working with a group of young players. During these sessions, I filmed a lot of the ball drills. I noticed that one guy was really struggling to catch the intermediate ball from 16 to 18 yards. It was as if the ball went through a blind spot; the player seemed to lose the ball then pick it up again. When he would pick up the flight of the ball again, the ball often got on top of him before he got a chance to react. As I continued to watch this kid, it was clear that he had a problem tracking the arc of the ball in that 15- to 18-yard area. We had his vision checked, and sure enough he had a condition that is common among some baseball players. They are able to pass a normal eye test, but they have trouble tracking the arc of a ball over a certain distance. Fortunately, this is a correctable condition; the kid had to do exercises to help strengthen the tracking ability of his eyes. Now the first thing I do when I get a new player is send him to get his eyes checked. It is amazing how many guys need contacts or glasses and never thought they needed them. Playing at the highest level is difficult without having the proper vision. Things happen quickly, and your judgment will be impaired without crystal clear vision.

As a player, you want to have your eyes checked every year. Coaches should not just assume that each player's vision is sound. Coaches may notice a player struggling with something that the player does not even realize is a problem. Coaches should trust what they see, especially if a player consistently reacts poorly to balls or if the ball seems to be sneaking up on him. The player may need to get his eyes checked.

Frame the Football With Proper Body Position

A receiver must have great agility and body control so he can get his body in the best position to be able to catch the ball. You need to get your body directly behind the ball whenever possible. While the ball is in flight, get your entire body—head, eyes, and hands—behind the direct flight of the ball (figure 5.1). Great body positioning means wherever the ball is, you get your whole body in the best position to make the play on the ball. If the ball is just above the ground, you must get your shoulders, hands, and eyes just above the ground so you can best make the catch (figure 5.2).

FIGURE 5.1   Getting the body behind the flight of the ball.

FIGURE 5.2   Getting low to the ground to catch a low ball.

FIGURE 5.3 Getting in position to catch a ball thrown behind you.

FIGURE 5.4 Improve upper-body flexibility by standing with hips open and catching a ball thrown behind you.

Upper-body flexibility is a key trait in catching the ball. The majority of balls are not thrown accurately. The receiver has to adjust and move his body into awkward positions to get his hands in position to catch a ball thrown behind him (figure 5.3). This is an important skill that some players do better than others.

Some players are stiff in their upper body and struggle to get their hands in position to catch balls thrown behind them. This is often seen in tight ends or fullbacks because they are bigger, stiffer athletes and have a difficult time adjusting to the ball.

One way to improve upper-body flexibility is to stand with your hips open and reach back to catch a ball thrown behind you (figure 5.4). This is more difficult for tight ends and fullbacks, guys who are a little more thick and muscular. They can practice getting their hands in position to catch the ball in this more awkward position by moving their hands around the body clock. Imagine the face of a clock on the upper body. The numbers of the clock represent the position at which the ball will be thrown. The ball can be thrown to these different areas to work on a player's upper-body flexibility.

Focus

Focus is the ability to block out all distractions in order to have single-minded concentration on the football. This is more natural for some players than for others. This skill separates the special players from the also-rans.

Concentration can be developed in practice. Repetition of distraction drills certainly helps. Players need to have other things going on while they zero in on catching the ball. They have to learn to block out all other movements to focus solely on the ball.

Working on simple eye–hand coordination can also help players improve their focus and concentration. This involves practicing the simple reaction of repeatedly putting the hands softly behind a moving target.

Backstopping the Ball

I spent two years with the great Fred Biletnikoff, the hall of fame receiver for the Oakland Raiders. Fred was the receivers coach the two years that I coached tight ends with the Oakland Raiders. I learned so much from Fred. He was a Super Bowl MVP, and he talked about catching the football as Mozart might talk about striking the piano keys.

Fred talked about the importance of getting your hands behind the football in flight and backstopping the ball. In baseball, a backstop or fence is behind the catcher so if the ball gets past the catcher, it doesn't go into the stands. That's exactly what the receiver is trying to do with his hands. As a receiver, you must get your hands all the way behind the ball with your fingers close enough together so the ball can't go through your hands. The ball should never go through the hands. At worst, the ball might hit the hands and drop straight down. You might be able to catch it off the bobble before it hits the ground. Backstopping the ball is stopping the momentum of the ball so it never goes through the hands. Again, at worst, the ball's momentum is stopped, and the ball can be caught after hitting the hands.

> **"The ball should never go through your hands. As a receiver, you should always work to get your hands behind the ball and backstop the football."**
>
> *Fred Biletnikoff, hall of fame receiver for the Oakland Raiders*

Whenever possible, try to get your eyes behind the hands on the flight of the ball. This is not always possible because of the position of some balls; however, when possible, having your eyes behind your hands improves your ability to see the ball all the way into your hands (figure 5.5).

Be a competitive catcher. Fred was the ultimate competitive catcher. He simply believed that he was supposed to catch every ball and that there

FIGURE 5.5 Getting the eyes behind the hands in order to see the ball all the way into the hands.

was no ball he couldn't catch. On the rare occasion when Fred would drop a pass, he would have someone throw that same pass to him over and over again after practice so that he wouldn't drop the same pass again.

I have the push-up rule. Every time a player drops a ball in practice, the player has to drop and do 10 fingertip push-ups. Fingertip push-ups are old school. They are great for hand strength, which is another positive reason for doing them. Fingertip push-ups help strengthen the fingers and the hands and protect players from getting the fingers jammed. I have always believed that this immediate punishment helps concentration.

Making the Catch

Catching the ball outside the framework of the body is an important skill (figure 5.6). One of the biggest benefits to executing the pat-and-go drill (see page 70) every day is that the quarterbacks and receivers learn to throw

FIGURE 5.6 A receiver catching the ball outside the framework of the body while putting his body between the defender and the ball.

and catch the ball outside the framework of the body. If players understand this skill, they will finish more big plays down the field over the course of the year. This skill (or lack of it) shows up all the time when teams throw deep. When the quarterback can consistently place the ball away from the defender, more completions will be made. When the receiver learns how to consistently keep his body between the defender and the football, he will either make the big catch or draw a pass interference penalty on his attempt to finish the play.

The back-shoulder throw is one of the most underutilized throws in the game, but the quarterbacks who can throw it effectively can really hurt defenders because it is nearly impossible to defend when thrown properly. The reason the back-shoulder throw is so tough to cover is because it is thrown while the defender has his back turned; he can't see the flight of the ball to defend it. The ball is thrown behind the defender so the offensive player can see it and adjust to it, but the defensive player is late to react. The fact that the defender can't see the ball to react makes this pass almost impossible to cover when executed properly. The pat-and-go drill (page 70) gives quarterbacks and receivers an opportunity to work on these throws daily. Many people work this drill without indicating which specific throws to make. By practicing the specific throws, every player develops the more difficult aspects of the passing game and is able to function at a higher level of execution. The key is to practice the throws on a regular basis. Remember, you get what you emphasize.

Catching the ball on the back hip is my favorite catching skill to drill because it happens so often. Every pass is not perfect; on a crossing route, when the receiver is running across the field on a dead run, the ball is often thrown behind him on his back hip. That receiver has to open his shoulders and his front hip to be able to catch the ball softly in his hands (figure 5.7). This happens often on the football field, and a receiver has to learn how to bend his body to get his hands in position to catch the football.

Spatial awareness is a big part of being an effective receiver. Most complete pass offenses try to attack the whole field, both horizontally and vertically. Some pass patterns are out breaking cuts designed to have the receiver catch the ball on the sideline. These out cuts are

FIGURE 5.7 Catching the ball on the back hip.

timing patterns for the quarterback that are meant to be thrown before the receiver even snaps his head around. The quarterback often throws the ball right on the boundary where no one can make a play on the ball except the offensive receiver. This is where a receiver must become adept at seeing the ball and simultaneously getting his feet down. Working a sideline toe tap is difficult because the player is doing two things at the same time. The receiver is often trying to track a fast-moving ball while running to the sideline, and he must catch the ball while simultaneously making sure that he has his feet clearly in the field of play. In pro football, the receiver must get two feet clearly in the field of play. In college football, only one foot has to be in play when the ball is caught for it to be called a legal catch. When we drill this skill at the college level, we have the players work to get two feet inbounds, because if they can get two feet in, then getting one foot in should be even easier in the game.

Repetition

The only way to be a great catcher is to catch. One of my favorite stories is about Larry Bird of the Boston Celtics. Bird is often called the greatest jump shooter in NBA history. One story about Bird says that as a kid he used to shoot 500 free throws every day before he went to school. Ted Williams is called the greatest hitter of all time. Williams was the last major-league player to hit over .400 in a season. According to some stories, Williams used to take batting practice until his hands would bleed. He was obsessed with hitting a baseball. He wanted to know more about hitting a baseball than anyone who ever lived.

Catching a football is a skill just like shooting a basketball or hitting a baseball. The more you do it, the better you get at it. College football players are restricted in how much time they can spend practicing every week. I used to chart practice and would find out that some of our best players would catch only 15 to 20 balls over the course of a 2 1/2-hour practice. Many times they wouldn't even catch that many balls in a practice. That's not nearly enough to become great. So I started throwing balls and shooting footballs from a Jugs machine to the players after practice. This too left me dissatisfied. We just weren't using our time well enough, and receivers were not catching nearly enough balls. That's when I discovered the tennis ball machines.

I first heard about the tennis ball machines from Mike Leach. Leach and Steve Spurrier Jr. used them at Oklahoma in 1999. Coach Leach used them at Texas Tech to help players build eye–hand coordination, and his teams broke a number of passing records. In 2010, the use of tennis ball machines became a part of our daily routine at Oklahoma. Now our receivers won't leave the field without catching 250 balls. A receiver can catch 250 balls in 10 minutes using the tennis ball machines. It's the best use of time for developing eye–hand coordination.

A tennis ball machine can be tilted to shoot at various angles and adjusted to shoot tennis balls at various speeds. Each machine can hold 50 to 60 balls at a time. We have 4- to 5-gallon buckets of tennis balls to refill each machine. Each player stands 7 to 10 feet away from the machine. As the balls begin to shoot out in a rhythmic fashion, the receiver catches them using one-hand catches. The receiver starts by catching 10 balls with his right hand, then 10 balls with his left hand. Then the receiver turns on his right side and catches 10 balls on the right, then switches and catches 10 balls on the left. He may then get down on a knee and catch over the right shoulder for 10, then switch and catch over the left shoulder for 10. The important thing is to change the angle and the type of catch every 10 to 15 repetitions. In all, each player catches about 250 balls in 10 minutes. The players could never catch that many in that amount of time on the Jugs machine, but this can be accomplished without the machines. A coach can simply use a 5-gallon bucket of balls, throw the balls one by one at the receiver, and have the receiver catch the balls at all the angles. We have found this to be just as efficient and an even faster way to get the 250 balls in after practice. It is a fabulous way for players to train to move their hands and eyes and pluck a moving target out of the air. Our guys will catch 1,000 balls over the course of a week—and that's just after practice. That type of repetition has an accumulative effect on a player's confidence. And a team needs confident, competitive ball catchers.

Pat-and-Go

The pat-and-go drill is usually done daily as a warm-up with the quarterbacks and the receivers. We typically do it before walk-through or stretch as a drill that enables the quarterbacks and skill players to loosen up. This drill helps the quarterbacks get their arms warm, and it helps the skill players get their legs warm.

SETUP: Quarterbacks start in the middle of the field. One quarterback starts on the 5-yard line and works out; the other starts on the 35-yard line and works in toward the goal line. Skill players stand in two lines, one line on the right side of each quarterback. Each line of receivers starts a couple yards outside the hash. There are no defenders in this drill.

EXECUTION:

1. The first receiver in line starts running when the quarterback pats the ball. The receiver runs the route, the quarterback throws the ball, and the receiver catches it. After catching the ball, the receiver runs down the field and gives the ball to the quarterback on the other end of the field. Then he joins the end of the receivers' line on that side of the field.

2. The receivers rotate through, running specific routes for the various rounds of the drill. The first round is quick slants.

3. The next set of routes is go balls. The key to the go ball is that the quarterback wants to work on putting the ball up and over the receiver's outside shoulder. In turn, the receiver wants to work on keeping his body inside the flight of the football and catching the ball on the outside framework of his body. On all go balls, this is where the quarterback wants to place the ball, and the receiver wants to get used to shielding the defender away from the ball with his body.

4. The next throw in the drill is a vertical back-shoulder throw. This is used on go balls when the receiver isn't beating his defender down the field. The quarterback throws the ball on a line right at the receiver's outside shoulder. This pass forces the wide receiver to adjust to a ball that is purposely thrown short and away from the defender, who, with his back turned, will be helpless to react to the ball.

COACHING POINTS: When this drill is done properly, the receiver should always put his body in between the ball and the imaginary defender. This technique will show up later in practice for the quarterback and the receiver on all go balls. This is a critical technique for all downfield balls, and we practice it every day in pat-and-go.

Quick Carioca Turn

I love the movement and agility of this drill. Each player must get his hips down and do a quick mini carioca with his back turned to the coach. This is a great agility drill as well as a great concentration and confidence drill. It's a great drill to do early in individual practice or on game day to get the players loosened up and ready to go.

SETUP: Receivers line up single file on the sideline, heading toward the hash. The first receiver in line turns his back to the coach.

EXECUTION:

1. One at a time, the players work the drill from the sideline to the hash mark.

2. On the coach's command "hit," the receiver does a quick mini carioca for about 4 yards with his back to the coach.

3. On the coach's "turn" command, the receiver snaps around and runs down the line. Simultaneously, the coach throws the ball as the receiver's head comes around.

4. The receiver must snap his head, find the ball, catch it, and then stride down to the hash.

5. Every player in line gets a repetition, and then the group works back from the hash for a second round.

COACHING POINTS: When working on any type of turn drill, a receiver should work the head and hands together in one piece. I want players to do a quick mini carioca so the feet are moving only a couple of inches and the hips and hands are moving with the feet. On the coach's command, the player must snap and whip his head and hands around to catch the football.

Catching the Ball on the Back Hip Drill

SETUP: Receivers line up in single file on the sideline. The coach lines up between the sideline and the numbers about 7 to 10 yards from the receivers.

EXECUTION:

1. One at a time, the receivers stride straight down the field toward the hash mark. The receiver strides at about half speed down the line toward the hash.

2. The coach throws the football on a line right at the receiver's front shoulder (figure 5.8a). If the coach throws the ball right at the receiver's front shoulder, the ball will be behind the receiver.

3. The receiver has to open his back hip and his upper body to get his hands in position to catch the ball (figure 5.8b).

4. Each player gets one catch working from the sideline to the hash mark.

5. Once each player has gone from the sideline to the hash mark, the whole group repeats the drill going back from the hash mark to the sideline. Each player will get two repetitions.

COACHING POINTS: Some players are more flexible in the upper body than others. All receivers need to get good at this drill because this type of pass happens a lot in the game. The drills that coaches use should reflect what happens most in the game! If it doesn't happen in the game, don't spend time practicing it, and don't create a drill for it. All drills must be done for a reason, and the reason should be that the drill involves action that occurs in the game and that the player must be prepared for.

FIGURE 5.8 Catching the ball on the back hip drill: *(a)* Coach throws at the receiver's front shoulder; *(b)* the receiver opens the back hip and upper body to catch the ball.

Sideline Toe Tap

SETUP: Receivers line up single file on the outside edge of the numbers. The coach is behind the line at a 45-degree angle, about 7 to 10 yards away, the same angle that a quarterback would be throwing at.

EXECUTION:

1. On the coach's cadence "hit," the receiver breaks full speed toward the sideline.

2. The coach lets the ball go right on the boundary so the wide receiver must catch the ball and get his feet down at the same time.

3. Each player gets a repetition over his right shoulder (figure 5.9a), and then the drill is flipped so each receiver catches a pass over the left shoulder (figure 5.9b).

4. The same drill can be used to work on a corner route. The wide receiver comes out at a deeper angle up the field.

COACHING POINTS: The receiver must see the ball and feel the sideline. Nothing matters if the receiver doesn't catch the ball. The most important thing is to catch the ball first and then worry about getting the feet inbounds. A saying that I use is "You have to see the ball and feel the boundary." Boundary awareness is the key in this drill. The receiver must learn to know where he is on the field without taking his eyes off the football.

FIGURE 5.9 Sideline toe tap drill: *(a)* catching the ball over the right shoulder; *(b)* catching the ball over the left shoulder.

Turn on Command Three Times

SETUP: Receivers line up single file. The first man in line has his back to the coach (figure 5.10a). The coach is 7 to 10 yards away from the receivers.

EXECUTION:

1. This is a stationary drill; players won't move from their starting spot.
2. On the coach's "turn" command, the receiver snaps (figure 5.10b) and catches (figure 5.10c).
3. The coach throws the ball just as the receiver is snapping around. The coach can move the ball around so the receiver has to catch high, wide, and tight. The coach can work around the face of a clock to make the receiver catch in different positions.
4. The receiver does this three consecutive times, then the next guy in line gets his turn.

COACHING POINTS: I like stationary drills that involve turning and catching because these drills help players build confidence and improve their ability to snap their head and eyes to find the ball. Again, the emphasis is on snapping the head and hands together. The other plus to this drill is that there is very little running involved. It's a good drill for working the hands and also saving the players' legs from too much running.

FIGURE 5.10 Turn on command three times: *(a)* Receiver stands with his back to the coach; *(b)* the receiver turns on the coach's command, and the coach throws the ball; *(c)* the receiver catches the ball.

Catch Behind the Goalpost

This drill is nothing new. In fact, it's as old as the hills but involves just another form of distraction using something every school has on its field—a goalpost. This is a simple drill that you can change up and do from different angles to change the view for the receiver.

SETUP: Receivers line up single file from the endline to 8 to 10 yards from the goalpost. The coach is in the end zone about 8 to 10 yards away, throwing balls to each receiver.

EXECUTION:

1. On the coach's command "hit," the first receiver strides on a straight line behind the goalpost (figure 5.11a).

2. The coach lets the ball go so the receiver must run behind the goalpost and catch the ball on the other side (figure 5.11b). Receivers want to work about 1 yard behind the goalpost so they don't run in to it.

3. The ball must travel through the receiver's blind spot, and he must pick up the ball's flight on the other side.

COACHING POINTS: The key to the drill is that the coach must time the throw so the receiver loses sight of it for a split second. Players will learn to track the flight of the football and will learn to pick it up quicker when they lose sight of it for a split second.

FIGURE 5.11   Catch behind the goalpost: *(a)* Receiver runs behind the goalpost; *(b)* coach throws the ball so the receiver runs behind the goalpost to catch it.

End-Zone High Ball

One of the greatest plays in NFL history was "The Catch." In the NFC championship game, Joe Montana rolled out and threw to Dwight Clark, and the young San Francisco 49ers beat the famed Dallas Cowboys. The play is one that every football fan has seen a thousand times: Montana rolls out to his right with Too Tall Jones coming after him. Just as he goes out of bounds, Montana lets the ball go to the back of the end zone. It looks as if the ball will go high out the back of the end zone, but out of nowhere Dwight Clark snatches the ball from the air and scores as the clock winds down. This is one of the most thrilling finishes in sports history. That's where this next drill comes from. This is an end-zone high ball drill. This drill is done in the end zone with a group of receivers.

"When I'm flushed from the pocket, my receivers do a good job of getting open. They adjust well to it. When you have guys who move when you move, it's hard to cover."

Hall of fame quarterback Joe Montana after "The Catch"

SETUP: Receivers line up 3 yards from the back endline, from the goalpost to the corner of the end zone.

EXECUTION:

1. The first receiver in line near the goalpost spins out and strides just inside the endline, moving along the back of the end zone toward the back corner of the end zone.
2. The quarterback snaps the ball on the 3-yard line and springs out toward the sideline.
3. The players standing at the back of the end zone hold their hands in the air to create a distraction.
4. The quarterback rolls out and throws the ball high to the back endline so the receiver has to go up and get the ball high (figure 5.12).
5. The receiver should go up and take the ball like a basketball player taking a rebound off the rim.

COACHING POINTS: This is a great red-zone drill for quarterbacks and receivers. These red-zone throws are specific throws that must be practiced separately and drilled specifically.

FIGURE 5.12 End-zone high ball.

High-Ball Drill

SETUP: Players work from the sideline to the hash. Players line up in single file right down a yard line. The coach stands 5 yards from the line of receivers on the sideline as well.

EXECUTION:

1. One receiver is designated as the offensive player, and the players on his right and left are the defensive distracters.

2. On the coach's "hit" command, all three players take off straight down the yard line toward the hash mark. Players must stride and not run all out.

3. As the players head toward the hash mark, the coach launches a high-angle throw that will travel in the air like a jump ball.

4. Tho offensive receiver must adjust to the flight of the ball and go up to get it at its highest point (figure 5.13). The two defensive distracters do not go after the ball, but they run alongside the offensive player with their hands up.

5. Repeat the drill until each player gets a turn as the offensive player.

COACHING POINTS: This is a great drill for teaching and emphasizing how to go up and attack the ball at its highest point. Players must know how to adjust to the ball on the run, and they must get used to gathering themselves on the run to go up and get the football before the defender makes a play on it. The offensive player must believe that whenever a pass is thrown, that is his football. All offensive players must go after the ball with that intent. It is similar to taking the ball off the rim for a rebound in basketball.

FIGURE 5.13 High-ball drill.

Vertical Ball Adjustment Versus Defensive Backs

SETUP: Quarterbacks are in the middle of the field flanked by a line of receivers on both their right and left. Receivers will go one at a time, one on one versus a bump-and-run defensive back. The defensive back can play press or off man.

EXECUTION:

1. On the snap of the ball, the receiver runs a go ball, and the quarterback throws the ball deep down the field.

2. Both the receiver and the defensive back work to get into position to make a play on the football.

3. Each receiver will get three or four repetitions.

COACHING POINTS: This is a highly competitive drill that is best done at the end of practice on a Tuesday. You can really see the athletic ability of the two athletes when they are in a dead sprint trying to make a play on the football! This is a great drill because, over the course of the practice, most players—especially quarterbacks, receivers, and defensive backs—don't get enough work on deep balls. They all need the extra work on this specific type of throw. The receiver should focus on giving the quarterback room on the outside to drop the ball over the outside hand. The receiver must not allow the defensive back to ride him toward the sideline. This becomes a battle of body position and technique. A lot of skill is on display in this drill, but running a go pattern also involves a lot of technique.

On Knees Low-Ball Drill

SETUP: Each player starts on his knees in an upright position. The coach is 5 to 7 yards away.

EXECUTION:

1. The coach throws three consecutive balls to each player. The ball is thrown low so the player has to get both hands under the ball before it hits the ground.

2. The receiver should catch each ball (figure 5.14*a*) and then curl up in a fetal position to protect the ball (figure 5.14*b*).

COACHING POINTS: This is a great way for a player to work on catching a low ball that he will have to go to the ground to secure. This shows him where his hands and shoulders need to finish for the low catch. A receiver needs to get his shoulders down in position on any low ball. The great emphasis on this drill is the finish. Not only does the player go to the ground but he must also turn and roll to protect the football. We even finish by having the receiver hold the ball up as if showing it to an official to indicate he has the ball secure at the end of the play.

FIGURE 5.14   On knees low-ball drill: *(a)* From his knees, the receiver catches the low ball before it hits the ground; *(b)* the receiver curls up into a fetal position to protect the ball.

Low Ball on the Run

SETUP: Receivers line up in single file on the sideline, working down a yard line. Each player will run from sideline to hash mark. The speed of the drill is a steady stride.

EXECUTION:

1. On the coach's command, the first player strides down the line.
2. The coach throws the ball low in front of the receiver so it arrives near the receiver's kneecaps.
3. On the run, the receiver has to get his hands in position with the pinkies together in order to get behind the ball and make the catch (figure 5.15).
4. Each player should get a repetition going toward the hash mark and then again back toward the sideline.

COACHING POINTS: This is another ball drill in which players work on balls thrown below the waist. On any ball thrown below the chest, the player should be sure to put his pinkies together. This is the proper hand position for catching a ball that is below the chest.

FIGURE 5.15 Low ball on the run.

Over the Shoulder

SETUP: Receivers line up single file on the sideline. The coach is 4 to 5 yards in front of the receivers. The first receiver is in a stationary position with his back turned to the coach.

EXECUTION:

1. Looking over his right shoulder, the first receiver simulates running by pumping his arms in a running motion.
2. The coach delivers three balls over the receiver's right shoulder.
3. The receiver then looks over his left shoulder. The coach delivers three balls over the receiver's left shoulder.
4. Each player should get three balls over each shoulder.

COACHING POINTS: This is a great drill for working on over-the-shoulder catches. It is a good drill to add in when guys are sitting around between periods in practice because it takes no running and each player can get several throws in a short amount of time.

Straight Over the Top

SETUP: Receivers line up single file on a horizontal yard line. Each player works from the sideline toward the hash mark. The coach is on the sideline.

EXECUTION:

1. Players go one at a time. On the coach's command, the receiver runs straight down the yard line toward the hash (away from the coach) without looking back.

2. From directly behind the receiver, the coach throws the ball high and directly over the top of the receiver's head back toward the hash mark (figure 5.16a).

3. The ball is thrown so the receiver has to pick up the ball in the air straight over the top of his head to catch the ball (figure 5.16b).

4. After the catch, the receiver turns and throws the ball back. Then, as the receiver is running back down the line toward his original alignment, the coach delivers another ball.

5. The player catches the second ball as he works his way back to his original alignment.

COACHING POINTS: One of the toughest catches to make is when the ball is thrown directly over the receiver's head and he can't pick up the flight of the ball until the last minute. This is also not an easy ball for the coach to throw. The coach must become skilled at delivering accurate passes to simulate all the different catches that a receiver has to make.

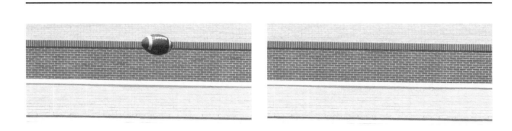

FIGURE 5.16 Straight over the top: *(a)* The coach throws the ball high over the receiver's head; *(b)* the receiver picks up the ball and catches it.

Knuckleball

SETUP: Receivers line up single file on the sideline on a yard line. Players work this drill from the sideline to the hash mark. The coach is directly in front of the first receiver.

EXECUTION:

1. On the coach's command, the first player runs directly toward the coach.

2. The coach grabs the football around the top of the tip and palms the top of the ball. The goal is to throw the ball like a pumpkin. The coach wants no spiral on it at all. He wants to throw a knuckleball that moves and jumps in the air and is difficult to catch.

3. When thrown properly, the ball will move erratically through the air, and the receiver will have to really concentrate to track the awkwardly moving ball.

COACHING POINTS: This is a creative drill that challenges the ball catcher to make tough catches. By challenging the player to catch the ball in an awkward position, the drill helps the player improve his eye–hand coordination.

Summary

The very essence of being a wide receiver is the skill of catching the football. In this chapter, we talked about how you can develop and refine that skill. The great receivers I have been around love to catch the ball. They have great pride in their ability to catch the ball. They believe they can catch the ball in any situation. The great players constantly do things on the field that defy the odds and make people scratch their head and say, "Wow, how did he do that?" Ball drills can be as creative as you can make them. Any drill that forces the player to concentrate when distracted and still focus to catch the football will improve the player's ball skills. Now that we have taken a deep look at the skill of catching the football, it's time to develop a plan for getting off bump-and-run coverage in order to get in position to catch the ball. Those release drills are the focus of the next chapter.

6

Releases

Having a plan for how to release off the football versus man coverage is what separates special players from average ones. Almost every player could run a 12-yard hook on air. But when an aggressive, fast defender is up on the line of scrimmage—a defender whose job is to bump and run and disrupt the receiver's every movement—then the receiver's ability to run that same 12-yard hook becomes a real challenge. You must have a plan of attack. You have to be able to see and recognize defensive technique. You must have skills and tools that you can apply when facing various techniques. I call that having tools in your tool kit. Plus, you must have the aggressive mind-set to think quickly and attack in hand-to-hand combat in order to separate from the defender. This is where the one-on-one battles are won and lost. This is a crucial skill for receivers to master because the most critical plays of any game are made in these one-on-one battles.

Releasing Versus an Off Technique

Get from point A to point B as fast as you can. The shortest distance between two points is a straight line. Everything receivers do should be to get from the line of scrimmage to their reception area point as fast as possible without deviation.

On all vertical routes, receivers should work on a straight line. A straight line is a line directly over the receiver's stance to a spot at the depth of his route. For example, if a receiver runs a 12-yard hook route and splits 2 yards outside the hash, the reception area for this route is 12 yards deep and 2 yards outside the hash (figure 6.1). This reception area is directly over the receiver's original alignment. The path from the receiver's starting point in his original stance to that reception area is a straight line. If the receiver travels that straight line, he covers the shortest distance, and it will take him the least amount of time to get there.

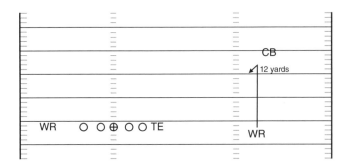

FIGURE 6.1   A 12-yard hook route with a split 2 yards outside the hash versus an off technique.

When a receiver runs a curl route versus an off technique, it is easy for the receiver to run a straight line because no defender is disrupting or imped-ing his course. His timing should be as if he were running this route on air. This changes when the defensive back walks up in a bump-and-run press technique and tries to bang and disrupt the receiver's route and timing.

Releasing Versus Press Coverage

Whenever a wide receiver aligns against a press technique, the elements of the game change. The timing and approach are different than when the defensive back is in off coverage. The biggest mistake a wide receiver can make against press coverage is to run a big wide arc to avoid contact (figure 6.2). He ends up running much farther on the hook route than he needs to, and it takes him much longer to get to his route depth and reception area.

Figure 6.2 shows an outside release by the wide receiver, who does a poor job getting back to his original alignment. In figure 6.3, the wide receiver does a better job releasing outside the press corner and then getting back over his original alignment.

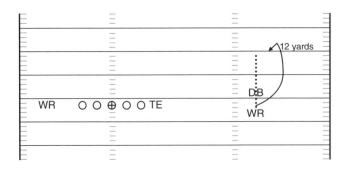

FIGURE 6.2   A 12-yard hook route with a split 2 yards outside the hash versus a press defender. The wide receiver runs too wide around the defender.

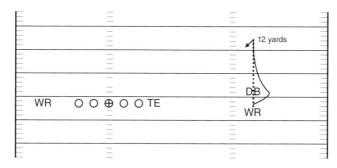

FIGURE 6.3 A 12-yard hook route versus a press defender. The wide receiver gets back over his original alignment.

Figure 6.4 shows an acceptable outside release against press coverage. The receiver starts outside the defender, who then slides in front of the wide receiver. The wide receiver slips back inside the corner. The key is that the wide receiver didn't release inside his original alignment. This is an acceptable release.

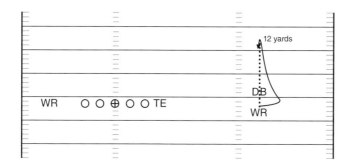

FIGURE 6.4 Acceptable outside release versus press coverage.

Understanding Defensive Backs

In my playing career, I played almost every position, from wide receiver to defensive back to tight end to linebacker. I finished my college career at the University of Iowa as an all-conference defensive back. In my senior year, I led the country in interceptions. As an offensive coach, I have always found it helpful to have this insight into the defensive mind-set. I understand what the defensive players are thinking, what they look for, and more important, what they are taught.

A defensive back lined up in a press technique has one job—to disrupt the route and destroy the timing and the route continuity between the quarterback and the receiver. The defensive back will try to disrupt the route by attempting to off-hand jam the receiver and flatten out his release, forcing him wide and off his alignment. The defender tries to throw off the timing of the routes with the quarterback. The defender wants to take away the quarterback's options so he has to hold the ball a split second longer until the rush can get to the quarterback. This is the never-ending battle between the wide receiver and defensive back in a press situation.

Against a press technique, the receiver needs to get back on that line. When the wide receiver takes his split and gets in his stance, he should imagine a vertical line that goes straight over his alignment. This is the line that the wide receiver wants to try to work on in all his routes. For the receiver to get from point A to point B as fast as possible, he must avoid the defender and get back on this line as quickly as he can.

Pass protection is everyone's responsibility, not just the offensive linemen's. The receiver's job is to get open as fast as possible before the rush gets to the quarterback. Against press technique, the most effective wide receivers are those who can avoid the press, get back on that line, and complete the route as quickly as possible. The ability to beat press coverage consistently separates good players from great players. In Major League Baseball, a player's inability to hit a curveball might keep him from reaching the big leagues. In the NFL, it's the inability to effectively beat bump-and-run technique that keeps young receivers from making an NFL roster.

> **"I had to be physical because the guys I played against were physical."**
>
> *Fred Biletnikoff, hall of fame receiver for the Oakland Raiders*

Reading the Triangle

The most important thing about releasing from press coverage is that you need to have a plan. You cannot form a plan until you first take in the necessary information. You can't form a release plan until you understand the technique and coverage responsibility that you are getting from the man over you. You have to understand secondary coverages. Your understanding of secondary coverages will tell you what to expect from the technique of the man over you.

To get the information he needs, a receiver should run through a checklist before the snap. We teach outside receivers how to read the triangle. The triangle refers to three players on the defense: the man over the receiver, the near safety, and the near linebacker (figure 6.5). These three defenders provide the information that the wide receiver needs in order to evaluate what to expect from the technique of the man over him.

The first indicator in the triangle is the man over you. You should first determine if this defensive back is lined up inside or outside of your alignment. If the defensive back is lined up outside, this is a big indicator of zone coverage. If the defender is lined up inside, this is a big indicator of man coverage. Next, you should determine if this defender is up on the line of scrimmage or off the line of scrimmage. Typically, a defensive back who is pressed up and inside is an indication of man coverage. If a defen-

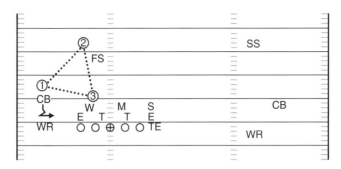

FIGURE 6.5 Reading the triangle (Cover 2): defensive man over receiver, near safety, and near linebacker.

sive back is off and outside, this is an indication of zone coverage. This information is important but is just part of the equation. The second part of the triangle provides a more complete idea of what type of reaction you will get from the secondary.

The next part of the triangle is the near safety. The near safety will give you an idea of what type of secondary support the corner will be getting in the coverage. Is the safety deep and outside the hash? If the safety is deep and outside the hash mark, there is a good chance the corner will roll up and cloud or press the receiver. When the safety gets in this position, he is in position to give the corner deep help, which frees the corner to play more aggressively and tighter on the receiver in the flat. This is a double-coverage position by the safety. So when the safety is deep and outside the hash, the receiver has to anticipate that the corner will jam him and play much more flat-footed. If the near safety is playing center field, he has the deep middle responsibility. When the near safety is in this position, the corner has no deep outside help. The receiver can anticipate the corner playing much more conservatively because he has no deep help. This is a single-coverage situation. If the near safety is short and in the near flat 5 or 6 yards from the line of scrimmage, this is a sky position, or a safety support position. This means the safety is getting in position to play the run. He does not have deep pass coverage responsibility. In this case, the corner would have no deep help from the near safety, so the receiver should anticipate the corner playing more conservatively in the short flats; again, this is a single-coverage situation.

The position of the corner over you and the safety will let you know what type of defense to expect. When the corner is up within 5 yards and the near safety is outside the hash, you can expect Cover 2. You should anticipate that the corner will bang and collide with you off the snap. Expect the corner to play physically because he has deep help from the safety. This is a form of double coverage.

In figure 6.6, the triangle is completely different. The corner is off, and the safety is deep in the middle of the field. This indicates some kind of Cover 3. You can expect single coverage. The corner will likely play you soft because he has no deep help.

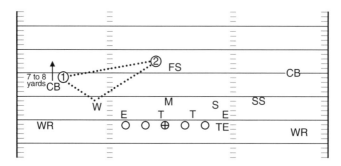

FIGURE 6.6 Reading the triangle (Cover 3): defensive man over receiver, near safety, and near linebacker.

The near linebacker is the third part of the triangle. The near linebacker can give a real indication of whether the defense is playing man or zone. If the near linebacker is off the line of scrimmage and in a soft position, that is a good indication of zone coverage. If the near linebacker is blitzing off the edge on the snap, this is a great indication that you may be getting man coverage.

Body Language

The defenders' body language is a huge indicator of what they are getting ready to play because certain body language is tied to certain kinds of coverage. This doesn't always hold true, but body language is often dead on. If the defenders are relaxed, standing on their heels (i.e., standing tall with their body weight back), and looking at the quarterback, there is a great chance that they are using zone coverage. If the defenders are nervous and jittery, bent over on their toes, and locked in on the receiver, there is a great chance that they are in man coverage. Typically, if the defenders are focused on the quarterback, that indicates zone. If each defender's eyes are locked in on his man, that is an indicator of man-to-man coverage.

Use Your Hands

The offense can and must use their hands. Youth coaches often tell kids that defensive players can use their hands but offensive players cannot; this is not true. This goes along with the myth that defensive players are more aggressive than offensive players. In my world, nothing could be further from the truth. First, the ability to use your hands is a skill that all football players must learn regardless of position. Second, offensive players need to play under control but also play aggressively. We want them to be the most physical players on the field, regardless of their position. The ability to use the hands along with an aggressive mind-set is essential to having the ability to get great releases off the line of scrimmage.

Imagine that your body has a cylinder around it. You don't need to worry about the defender until he invades your cylinder and tries to put his hands on you. If the defensive back tries to put his hands on your body above the chest, you should use a circular forearm pull to deflect his hand (figure 6.7a). We call this movement high hands or forearm pull. In the movie *The Karate Kid,* they called it wax off. If the defender tries to touch you below the waist, take the open hand straight down his jersey in one movement to deflect the defender's hands (figure 6.7b). We call this movement cleaning your pads.

FIGURE 6.7 Receiver using his hands to deflect a defender: *(a)* high hands when defender tries to touch you above the chest; *(b)* clean your pads when the defender tries to touch you below the waist.

The two-hand shove and quick swim move (figure 6.8) is a physical release that cuts right to the chase of what the receiver is trying to do. The wide receiver executes a two-hand shove on the defensive back right off the ball and then uses a quick swim move with a club and punch to swim over the defender's hands. This is an aggressive offensive release in which the wide receiver is not playing passively for the defender but is coming off the ball and creating space for himself to run upfield.

Arm over is a movement in which the defender sticks his arm out to slow the wide receiver and the receiver counters this action with an arm-over adjustment. Typically, this move is used when the defender's hand is chest high or lower. The wide receiver uses his hand to counter with a swimming motion over the top of the defender's hand (figure 6.9). In one continuous motion, the receiver pulls the defender by on the follow-through.

FIGURE 6.8 Two-hand shove and quick swim.

FIGURE 6.9 Wide receiver counters the arm-over movement by using a swimming motion over the defender's hand. This swimming motion or arm-over adjustment is an effective reaction for a receiver when the defender shoots a high hand.

Inside and Outside Releases

Inside and outside are the two directions of releases. In most offenses, the passing game will have designated routes. Each route may have a designated release that corresponds with it. In this section, we cover inside and outside releases. Understanding these releases allows players to make split-second decisions on the field so they can execute properly. Players need to know what is acceptable and what is not acceptable.

Inside Release

An inside release (figure 6.10)—on a crossing route, for example—is any release that is inside to over a receiver's alignment. This means that when the receiver gets into his stance and comes off the ball, he goes inside his alignment to over his alignment in order to get into his route. Going outside his alignment is not acceptable. On a crossing route, if the receiver is outside his alignment, he will have difficulty getting over to the other side of the field to execute his assignment.

An inside release does not necessarily mean that the receiver must release inside the defender playing over him. An inside release means a release that goes inside to over the receiver's original alignment. So a receiver could come off inside, and the defender could jump inside the receiver and cut him off. At that time, if the receiver adjusts and releases outside the defender but not outside his original alignment (figure 6.10b), this would be an acceptable inside release.

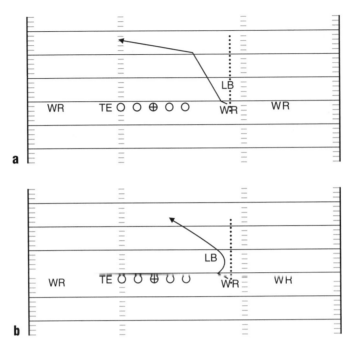

FIGURE 6.10 Inside release on a crossing route: *(a)* release inside the defender; *(b)* release outside the defender.

Outside Release

An outside release goes outside to over the receiver's original alignment (figure 6.11). A go route is a pattern that has an outside release. We want an outside release on a go ball because whenever we throw the ball vertically downfield, we don't want the safety to be a factor in making a play on the ball. We want to keep the ball as wide to the outside of the field as possible. If the receiver starts outside and the defensive player jumps outside to jam him, the receiver slips back inside the defender (figure 6.11*b*).

Cover 2 Release

Releasing versus a Cover 2 corner, or a clouded corner (figure 6.12), is one of the most common zone releases in football. Typically, cloud corners are taught to funnel the receiver back to the inside. The best plan of attack for the receiver releasing vertically on a cloud corner is to widen the corner by attacking his outside hip and threatening to release outside. Once the corner slides outside to protect and force the receiver inside, the receiver will have a clear release up the field. The wide receiver widens the corner on the snap by turning his shoulders on an angle off the line of scrimmage. Once the corner moves off his original alignment, the wide receiver can slip him upfield.

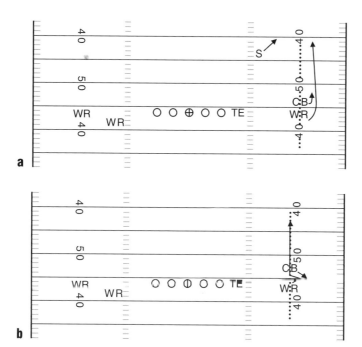

FIGURE 6.11   Outside release on a go route: *(a)* Receiver releases outside the corner; *(b)* receiver releases inside the corner but stays outside his original alignment.

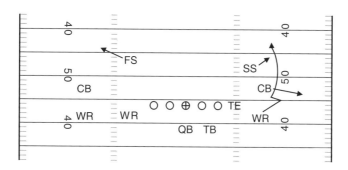

FIGURE 6.12   Release versus a Cover 2 corner.

Get the Defender on Train Tracks

After the wide receiver has gone by the defensive back and is running upfield, he should get totally on top of the defensive back. The phrase we use is "getting him on train tracks." This is a position where it appears as if both men are running on train tracks. The defensive back is totally left in a trail mode here. Remember, the wide receiver wants to be as open as possible to make the quarterback's job easier. The more a receiver can do this, the more opportunities he will get to catch the ball.

Jab Step

SETUP: Wide receivers line up in single file on the sideline. They will work horizontally across the field from the sideline to the hash. A pop-up dummy is set in front of the first wide receiver in line. The dummy is right in front of the receiver, simulating a bump-and-run defensive back.

EXECUTION:

1. On the coach's cadence "hit," the wide receiver performs a jab step and head-and-shoulders fake to release off the ball. The ball is off to the right or the left of the receiver, wherever the coach chooses.

2. The coach leans the dummy in the direction of the fake away from the wide receiver's release.

3. After he releases past the dummy, the wide receiver works to finish at the near hash mark.

4. All the wide receivers work to the hash to finish. The whole line can then work back in the other direction.

COACHING POINTS: Release drills should always be done on a vertical line so the wide receiver has a landmark on which to work vertically. After the receiver releases on the dummy, he can use the line as a landmark and try to get back on the line as quickly as he can. The jab step is a simple movement that receivers use more than you might think. From his stance, the wide receiver takes one clean, quick jab step with a head-and-shoulders fake and releases vertically off that one quick movement. The best way to release and beat a press defender is to never let him get his hands on you.

Stationary Hands (High and Low)

SETUP: Wide receivers partner up and take a position across from each other. One side of the line is on offense, and the other side is on defense. All players can go together; everyone works at once.

EXECUTION:

1. The defensive player stands at arm's length and tries to touch the offensive player's shoulder.

2. The defensive player should be methodical with his hand movements. He must not try to fool the offensive player with his hand movement.

3. When the defender's hand comes in high, the offensive player should pull it away with the forearm.

4. After several high-hand deflections, the defensive player should try to touch the offensive player's hip.

5. The offensive player now cleans his pads down the front of his jersey with an open hand to wipe the defender's hand off him.

6. After working high hands and then working low hands, the defender should work up and down on the coach's command.

7. After some good repetitions, players switch roles.

COACHING POINTS: Stationary hands is a good introductory drill for teaching wide receivers how to use their hands to keep defenders off them. It's best to introduce the drill in the off-season or early in training camp. This is a great drill because it focuses on the upper body and does not include any running.

Two-Hand Shove and Quick Swim

SETUP: Wide receivers form a single line across from a coach who has hand shields. The coach stands in good football position with his hands out front, thumbs to the sky. The coach is simulating the defender in this drill.

EXECUTION:

1. On the command "hit," the wide receiver comes off the ball with a two-hand shove to get the defensive back (the coach) on his heels.

2. In the next instant, the coach puts his hands on top of each other to allow the wide receiver to quick swim to the right.

3. The coach has the receiver repeat the shove phase and then perform a swim move to the left.

4. On the second swim move, the wide receiver should continue to release downfield to finish the drill.

COACHING POINTS: This is the first complete release move that I teach players. It is an aggressive offensive release in which the wide receiver is not playing passively for the defender but is coming off the ball and creating space for himself to run upfield. If the receiver learned only one move to get off the line of scrimmage, this would be it.

Arm Over

SETUP: The coach aligns over the wide receivers, who are in a single-file line. The coach has hand pads. The wide receivers are working on a vertical line.

EXECUTION:

1. On the movement of the wide receiver, the coach extends a single hand to the midsection of the oncoming wide receiver.
2. The wide receiver uses the arm-over move with the near arm and finishes with a follow-through as he works back on the line.
3. The wide receiver comes back the other way and works the move with the other hand in the other direction.
4. On the second move, the receiver should finish the release to bypass the coach.

COACHING POINTS: When the defender sticks his arm out to slow the wide receiver, the wide receiver counters with a swimming motion over the top of the defender's hand. In one continuous motion, the receiver pulls the defender by on the follow-through.

Forearm Pull Three Times

SETUP: This drill is similar to training performed by a boxer. The wide receiver stands with his elbows in and his hands high.

EXECUTION:

1. The coach must be very deliberate in his movement. He must not try to fool the wide receiver.
2. The coach reaches out to touch the wide receiver's shoulder. He reaches out three times—right, left, right.
3. The wide receiver performs a short forearm pulling movement to deflect the coach's hand.
4. The coach should stay in rhythm and go slowly until the wide receiver is used to the eye–hand movement.
5. The rhythm should be right—left-right; right—left—right; and right-left-right.
6. The wide receiver must get used to hitting moving targets.

COACHING POINTS: I came up with the forearm pull drill when I was working with the Indianapolis Colts. I'll never forget watching a playoff game between the Buffalo Bills and the Miami Dolphins. The Bills had an all-pro receiver named Eric Moulds. He was a strong, fast wide receiver with good upper-body strength. Miami played bump-and-run coverage the whole game. On this day, Moulds killed them by using this particular forearm pull technique. The Miami defensive backs stood right in front of the wide receiver as close as they could with their hands up. As soon as the ball was snapped, the defensive back put his hands right to the wide receiver's shoulder pads. Moulds would come off with low pads and high hands and pull his way off the football with a strong forearm pull. What I learned is that when a receiver has low pads, he can come off the ball with strength. When a receiver has high hands, he can work his hands and keep the defense from holding him.

Forearm Pull on the Side

SETUP: The coach uses hand pads and stands to the side of the wide receiver.

EXECUTION:

1. The coach puts pressure on the wide receiver's shoulder (figure 6.13a). The wide receiver pulls the coach's hand down (figure 6.13b) three consecutive times.

2. Each time the wide receiver pulls off the coach's hand, the coach returns the open hand pressure to the wide receiver's shoulder.

COACHING POINTS: Once a wide receiver releases past a defensive back, the defensive back will try to put his hand on the receiver's shoulder to slow the receiver down. The wide receiver must learn to pull that hand off his side. We do the forearm pull drill three times from the side. The key is that the receiver needs to pull himself back on top of his original alignment and get the defensive player in a trail position.

FIGURE 6.13 Forearm pull on the side: *(a)* Coach puts pressure on the wide receiver's shoulder; *(b)* the wide receiver pulls the coach's hand down.

Chop on Side Three Times

SETUP: Holding hand pads, the coach stands beside the wide receiver.

EXECUTION:

1. The coach puts pressure on the wide receiver's hip. The coach wants to apply pressure to the player's hip with the palm of his hand turned up.

2. When the wide receiver feels pressure, he chops the hand off. This chop is a violent downward movement by the receiver with the hand balled up. It is a violent downward stroke to get the opponent's hand off the receiver's body.

3. This movement is done three times right (figure 6.14a) and three times left (figure 6.14b).

4. The chopping movement is similar to trying to hammer a nail into a wall when leaning back against the wall.

COACHING POINTS: Once the wide receiver gets upfield and is side by side with the defensive back, the next thing that the defensive back will do is to look back and put his hand on the wide receiver's hip. The wide receiver must not allow the defensive back to slow him down by putting his hands on him all the way down the field. As soon as the wide receiver feels this, he must chop the hand off. This is not a finesse move; it is a violent action. The offensive player is physically chopping the defender's hand off his body!

FIGURE 6.14 Chop on side three times: *(a)* chop to the right; *(b)* chop to the left.

Pull, Pull, Chop

SETUP: Receivers line up in single file on the sideline. The coach holds hand pads and lines up over the wide receivers.

EXECUTION:

1. The first wide receiver releases with low pads and high hands (figure 6.15a).
2. When the wide receiver releases, the coach tries to put his off hand on the wide receiver's shoulder.
3. The wide receiver simultaneously tries to pull the coach's hand off (figure 6.15b).
4. While moving with the wide receiver, the coach again tries to place his hand on the wide receiver's shoulder.
5. Again, the wide receiver simultaneously pulls the hand off (figure 6.15c).
6. As the wide receiver starts to go by the coach, the coach should try to put his hand on the wide receiver's hip.
7. Simultaneously, the wide receiver should chop the coach's hand off as he goes by (figure 6.15d). The action is pull, pull, chop.
8. Then, as always, the wide receiver should work to get back on the vertical line.

COACHING POINTS: Release drills should always be worked on a vertical line so the wide receiver can see how tight he can stay to the line with as little deviation as possible. The best players can work to avoid contact on release and then get back on that line as quickly and with as little deviation as possible. This is a variation of the forearm pull three times but is a full release movement. The pull, pull, chop motion that the wide receiver does in this drill is a movement that happens all the time. Any defensive back in a bump-and-run technique will use an off-hand jam.

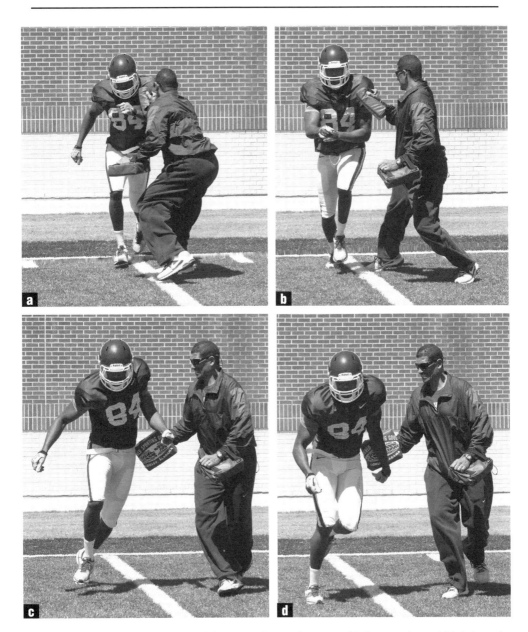

FIGURE 6.15 Pull, pull, chop: *(a)* The receiver releases with low pads and high hands; *(b)* the receiver pulls the coach's off hand off his shoulder; *(c)* the receiver pulls the coach's hand off his shoulder a second time; *(d)* the receiver chops the coach's hand off his hip while going past the coach.

Lateral Avoid Release

SETUP: Receivers stand in a single-file line on the sideline. They will work on a horizontal yard line, from sideline to hash mark. The coach holds hand pads and lines up over the wide receivers to simulate a defensive back. The wide receiver stands flat-footed on the line of scrimmage with his body balanced in his stance.

EXECUTION:

1. On the snap of the ball or the wide receiver's movement, the coach shoots both hands at the wide receiver's neck and chest to try to stop the wide receiver right on the line of scrimmage (figure 6.16a).
2. The wide receiver should read the coach's body language and balance his body weight up.
3. The wide receiver moves sideways or even slightly backward to totally avoid contact with the coach (defensive back) (figure 6.16b).
4. Once he avoids initial contact, the wide receiver escapes upfield and gets back on the vertical line, completely leaving the coach (defensive back) behind.

COACHING POINTS: This release should be used when the defensive back is trying to grab the receiver and quick jam him on the line of scrimmage. That's why the receiver needs to get a presnap read on the defensive back. The defensive back will often tip this tactic because he will almost always use it when he has deep help. Also, he will tip with his body language; he may be heavy and flat-footed and lean his body forward. The wide receiver must balance his body weight in his stance. He can even rise up slightly, making it easier to move laterally from side to side. The key is to get out of the way of the lunging defensive back trying to grab the receiver around the neck. The receiver wants to make him miss completely. If the receiver can make him miss, it's a huge play because this is a complete sell-out technique by the defender. When the receiver makes him miss, the receiver will be running free on air.

FIGURE 6.16 Lateral avoid release: *(a)* The coach reaches with both hands for the receiver's neck and chest to stop the receiver on the line of scrimmage; *(b)* the receiver moves laterally to avoid contact with the coach.

In, Out, In, Release

SETUP: Receivers stand in a single-file line on the sideline. Each receiver will work from the sideline to the hash on a horizontal yard line. The coach acts as the defender. He lines up in a bump-and-run position in front of the receiver.

EXECUTION:

1. The receiver comes off the ball and gives a quick inside lateral move.
2. The receiver's second move is an outside lateral move, trying to get the defender (coach) to jump him.
3. The third move is back inside and up the field vertically, beating the defender.

COACHING POINTS: This is a change-up move that a receiver can use on the defensive back. The whole premise is that most of the time the defensive back will jump on the second move that a receiver makes. So If the receiver ultimately wants to release inside, he should start with an initial move inside and then fake outside to get the defender to jump on his second move. When the defender takes the bait, the receiver steps back inside and takes the inside release.

Release in a 5-Yard Alley

SETUP: This is a group drill that should be done versus the defensive backs. The receivers stand in a single-file line at the sideline; they will work from the sideline to the hash mark. Both the receivers and defenders go one at a time. The receiver starts on the sideline and right in the middle of two adjacent yard lines going across the field.

EXECUTION:

1. The receiver releases past the defender from the sideline to the hash.
2. The defender tries to slide and collide to hold up the receiver.
3. The receiver must stay between the two adjacent yard lines. The receiver has a 5-yard cylinder in which to work in order to win his release.

COACHING POINTS: This is a great controlled drill for receivers and defensive backs alike. Each receiver must work on moving the defender and using his hands to swim and club by the defender. The drill is challenging for the receiver because it is done in a contained area. The receiver really needs to concentrate on his technique and fundamentals.

Summary

Releasing off press coverage is the most challenging skill that a receiver has to master. It is probably the most misunderstood part of the game. Most of the drills in this chapter come from years of observing and working with great players and coaches. These drills have stood the test of time. Remember, there is no single correct way to release off the ball versus press man coverage. These techniques should be thought of as different tools in a player's tool kit—tools that the player can pull out and apply when necessary. The ability to release leads the receiver into the wonderful world of route running, where personal expression really comes into play. That is the subject of the next chapter.

7
Route Running

I visited the Philadelphia Eagles when Jon Gruden was the offensive coordinator. They were working routes on air with the quarterbacks and wide receivers. As the guys went through their route progressions, Gruden said that route running was expression. He told the receivers that when they run a great route, they use their own personal expression and body movement to get open. They put their own stamp on the movement. It may be a look, a lean, or a nod that is unique to each receiver. It can't always be coached or explained, but I know what it looks like when I see it, and I can point it out to others. We explore the expression of route running in this chapter as well as the use of body control.

Earning Respect

First, you must get the defender's respect. As discussed in the last chapter, if you want to get open, you must run full speed. You have to come off the football and make the defender fear that you are going to run right by him. You have to get the defender's respect right from the snap. He has to think that you may run right by him on any given play. For route running, I teach only one speed—full speed! This really simplifies your thought process when you are running routes. By running full speed, you can eat up the cushion of the defender as quickly as possible.

Your eyes gain respect. Body language is important in life, and it's the same in football. A person who walks into a room, drifts off by himself, and keeps his eyes down to the ground will be seen by others as shy and will not be taken very seriously. But a person who walks confidently into a room, walks right up to people, and looks them directly in the eye will demand respect.

It's the same on the football field. A wide receiver who comes off the ball and runs away from the defender with his eyes on the ground will get no respect from the defense. The wide receiver who explodes off the football, runs right at the defensive back, and looks right through him will get immediate respect. The defensive back cannot help but turn and run because he must respect the fact that this wide receiver may run right by him. The use of vertical eyes sells deep routes. When the wide receiver's eyes are down, this makes it look as if he is running a short or intermediate route. A wide receiver has to play as if he is standing in front of a full-length mirror; he should always be aware of what he looks like to the defender.

Thinking Like a Defensive Back

Receivers must learn to think like a defensive back. Receivers must understand what is going on in the defender's mind. You cannot formulate a plan to beat the defensive back unless you know how he thinks or what he has been taught. To be able to attack the defender properly, you have to know what he is afraid of and what he is protecting.

Every defensive back is afraid to get beat deep, especially if he has no deep help. If you want to get open short, you must sell to the defensive back that you are going deep. You can run any route and get open by attacking the defensive back and threatening him one way and working the other. The defensive back's alignment will tell you how he is playing you and where his help is coming from. For example, if the defensive back is lined up inside you, he's been taught not to let you inside. You can take advantage of that by running toward a spot inside the defensive back's position, and in turn, he will allow you free access straight up the field. That's part of playing smart, and we will talk more about that when we explore reading coverages.

Great route runners are very detailed. You must have great awareness to be a great route runner. You must have a great understanding of the defensive mind-set. Defensive backs play percentages; they know that certain routes happen more on certain down-and-distance situations. They will play your split. If your split is tight, they will think you are running an out breaking route. If your split is too wide, they'll think you are going to run an in breaking route. On third and 4 or 5, they will be looking for the slant route in a blitz situation. As a receiver, you have to be aware of how the defensive backs think in these situations because you can put that information to work for you in those very same formations. As a wide receiver, you will find that the more you can make things look the same, the tougher it will be for the defenders to get a bead on you. The more you can keep your split consistent, the better off you are. Be aware of your eyes; never look at your break point. If you hurt a defensive back with a route earlier in the game, talk to the coaches about running a double-move route off the same stem later in the game.

Wide receivers should talk to the quarterback early in the game. A lot of things happen early in a football game. After the first series, the wide receivers should come off the field and talk about what happened in that series. The receivers should let the quarterback know how the defensive backs are playing them. I don't mean what coverages; I mean information such as whether the defenders are playing loose or not respecting the receivers deep at all. Sometimes teams come in and try to be really aggressive early. They play a lot tighter than they have in their previous games. This is why it's important for the offensive players to get on the same page after the first series. When teams play in a no-huddle offense, this kind of communication often has to take place between series because the players don't have the opportunity to exchange this information in the huddle.

Focusing Downfield

When coming off the ball and running your route, you should always have your eyes downfield. When the wide receiver's eyes are downfield, this gives the defensive back the impression that the wide receiver is pushing the route vertically. If the defensive back thinks the wide receiver is pushing the route vertically, this will help the wide receiver create more space on his intermediate routes.

Changing Direction

When you are changing direction and planting your feet while route running, you should keep your pads over your toes on your breaks (figure 7.1). This will help you change direction and will help you drop your center of gravity so you can accelerate out of your breaks and create separation at the top of the route.

Receivers should always come back to the football. When the wide receiver gets to his break point at the top of the route and the ball is in the air, he must make it a habit to come back to the ball. Defensive backs are taught to attack the football when it is in the air. Our philosophy is that when we throw the football, it is our ball—and we need to go after every ball in the air with that mind-set. At the top of the route, the wide receiver plants and comes back to the football to attack the ball with his hands. The great wide receivers are really good at this. Even when these receivers are

FIGURE 7.1 When breaking, a receiver should keep the pads over the toes.

covered, the quarterback will often still throw the ball to them because the quarterback trusts the wide receiver to come back to the ball.

Agility is important when you are running routes. Quick feet are a plus for getting in and out of your breaks as a receiver. Remember that the hands and feet should work together. When you pump your hands quickly up and down, this helps you fire your feet quicker in and out of your breaks. This becomes important at the top of your route, especially at the breaking point. Some wide receivers have a bad habit of stopping their hands as they get to their break point. The key is to continue to pump your hands and accelerate the feet as you go into your break.

The subtle moves will help you get open. Defensive players rely a lot on their instincts. Defensive players are primarily reactive players. They react to formations, to down and distance, and to body movements of the players they cover. As a wide receiver, you have to be aware of how your movements affect the defenders who cover you. The longer you play, the more you will realize all the little things you can do to throw off the defense. The great players pay attention to these things. With experience, you begin to realize that the subtle moves are the ones that get you open. A simple angle of the receiver's shoulders can open the defensive back's hips and allow the receiver to cross the defensive back's face. A simple glance or look away can draw the defensive back's attention away from your intended break. To be a great wide receiver, you must pay attention to how you can affect the defensive back with your little movements.

Routes

The following sections describe our favorite routes for attacking the defense. The routes are organized into three categories: quick game, intermediate, and drop back. The names of the routes refer directly to the area of the field that the routes attack.

Quick-Game Routes

Quick-game routes usually attack 5 to 6 yards from the line of scrimmage. Generally, the quarterback takes a three-step drop if he is under center. If the quarterback is in the shotgun, he may take only one step to properly time these patterns.

5-Yard Hitch

A 5-yard hitch route (figure 7.2) is a pattern that is run versus off coverage. On all our routes, receivers start with the inside foot forward in the stance. The front foot is up so the receiver can count his steps on certain routes to time them correctly.

The receiver takes three big steps and two short steps to get to a depth of 5 yards. The receiver comes around in one piece at 5 yards.

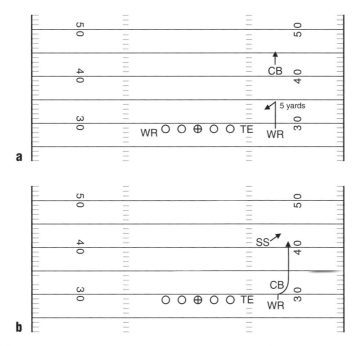

FIGURE 7.2   *(a)* 5-yard hitch route versus off coverage; *(b)* conversion versus rotation.

This route would convert versus rotation (Cover 2; figure 7.2*b*) or press coverage. The hitch converts to a fade versus press or rotation.

I like to call the hitch route a 5-yard takeoff. This means I want the receiver to explode off the ball and run as hard as he can for 5 yards. This will cause the defender to back off and give the receiver great separation. As a result, when the receiver catches the ball, he can turn on the defender and have the opportunity to make more yards.

The biggest mistake that players make is thinking they don't have to run hard because they are going only 5 yards. When the receiver comes off the ball at half speed, the defender doesn't feel threatened and will close on the ball. This often results in no gain if the pass is caught, or the defender may be able to break up the pass completely.

Three-Step Slant Route

The slant route (figure 7.3) starts with the inside foot forward in the stance. The receiver explodes off the ball with three steps at full speed. On the third step, the receiver plants and presses inside on a 45-degree angle. The receiver should take whatever angle he needs to beat the defender to the ball.

This route will adjust to a 5-yard hitch route versus off coverage with the same rules as described previously for the hitch. Versus press or rotation, the slant is a three-step route. The receiver plants the outside foot on the third step.

This route has many variations. After years of including this route in our offense, I am convinced that we have settled on the best way to run the

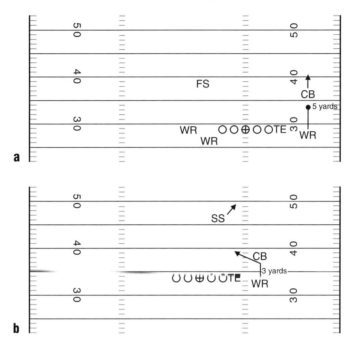

FIGURE 7.3   Three-step slant route: *(a)* converts to a hitch versus off coverage; *(b)* stays a slant versus press or rotation if defender is within 5 yards of the line of scrimmage.

route with the hitch conversion versus off coverage. The big emphasis on the slant route is that when the receiver comes off the ball, he must adjust the angle of the route to the defender's technique. If the defender is playing an inside technique, the receiver should run directly at the defender and break at whatever angle he needs to in order to beat the defender inside to the ball. That means that the angle of the route is directly related to the defender's technique.

How does a receiver read whether the coverage is off or not? As a rule, if the defender is within 5 yards of the line of scrimmage, the receiver should treat it as press or rotation and run the slant. If the defender is dropping with his hips turned and running downfield, the receiver should treat it as off coverage and run a hitch. Anytime the corner is deeper than 5 yards from the receiver, the receiver should run a hitch. If the defender is in a grey position, the receiver should always run a slant.

Quick Out

For the quick out (figure 7.4), the receiver explodes off the ball full speed for two full steps (he begins with the inside foot up in the stance). On the third step, the receiver uses an angle step and rolls over flat at 5 yards, running to the boundary. The head and hands come around in one piece.

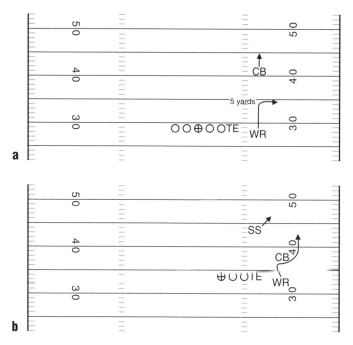

FIGURE 7.4   Quick out: *(a)* versus off technique; *(b)* converts to a fade versus Cover 2.

This is a full-speed route. If the receiver comes off at full speed, he will make the corner back off. This enables the receiver to gain separation from the defender so he has room to make more yards when he catches the ball.

The quick out converts to a fade versus press coverage or rotation (Cover 2; figure 7.4*b*).

Intermediate Routes

Intermediate routes are the meat and potatoes of the passing game. These are 8- to 12-yard timing patterns, go-to concepts that must be repeated again and again until they can be executed perfectly.

12-Yard Curl or Hook Route

The curl route (figure 7.5) is a full-speed 12-yard route. With the inside foot up, the receiver explodes off the ball to 12 yards downfield. At 12 yards from the line of scrimmage, the receiver drops his hips and, with the shoulders over the feet, plants on his outside foot. He bursts and turns to come straight back to the quarterback. On the curl route, the receiver must work back to the quarterback and the football.

The receiver must always get his depth with his outside foot. The receiver should always put that plant foot at 12 yards from the line of scrimmage. If the receiver plants and comes back to the quarterback but he can't see the quarterback, he should slide to the next inside window (figure 7.6). We have an old

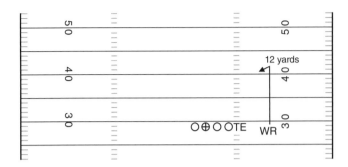

FIGURE 7.5 The 12-yard curl or hook route.

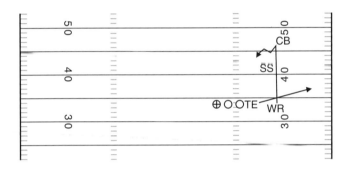

FIGURE 7.6 On a 12-yard curl route, the receiver works to the next inside window if he can't see the quarterback at the top of the break.

saying that if you can't see the quarterback, he can't see you either. When this happens, the receiver must slide to the next open window in the coverage.

12-Yard Out Cut

The 12-yard out cut (figure 7.7) is a pure timing route. With the inside foot up, the receiver runs a seven-step rollover out cut. The first six steps are straight up the field. The seventh step is an angle step at approximately 9 yards. The eighth step rolls over at around 10 yards. The top of the route is at 12 yards. The receiver works flat and back downhill at the top of the route. Versus rotation or press coverage, we convert this route to a fade (figure 7.7b).

The out cut is a pure timing route that must be perfected over many repetitions. We work hard to get all receivers to run this route the same way. The receiver must come off the ball and sell the go ball. Receivers should look right through the defender to get him to back off them. When I was with the Oakland Raiders, Al Davis used to talk about receivers having "vertical eyes." This means that the receiver's eyes are downfield. The receiver's eyes give the impression to the defender that he is going deep.

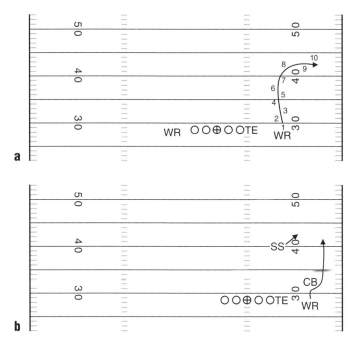

FIGURE 7.7   *(a)* 12-yard out cut; *(b)* converts to a fade versus rotation.

Drop-Back Patterns

For drop-back patterns to be successful, the offensive line must give the quarterback and receivers time to set up the routes. Solid drop-back patterns include the 16-yard dig and 16-yard comeback, the 12-yard post, the go ball, and the fade route.

16-Yard Dig Route

The 16-yard dig route (figure 7.8) is a way to get the ball into the 16- to 18-yard area. To get into this area, the receiver must use vertical speed up the field.

The receiver accelerates upfield with vertical speed. He drops his hips and plants his outside foot at 16 yards. The receiver plants and comes flat

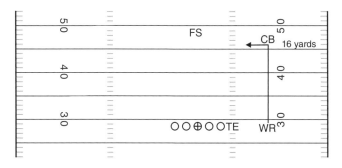

FIGURE 7.8   The 16-yard dig route.

across the field at a depth of 16 yards. At the top of the route, he may even press back toward the ball.

The reception area for the dig route is outside the hash. The route must not get too close to an inside safety who could make a play on the ball.

16-Yard Comeback

The 16-yard comeback (figure 7.9) is another vertical route that takes real speed by the receiver up the field. This route works the outside portion of the field. This is an individual route that works solely on the cornerback on the outside portion of the field. A receiver who is a vertical threat and can run a great comeback will be able to work a cornerback over into the boundary.

Every route works off the go ball. When the receiver can threaten to go deep on the go ball, he makes the defender respect the fact that he can get by him. In turn, this allows the receiver to be a threat on the comeback route.

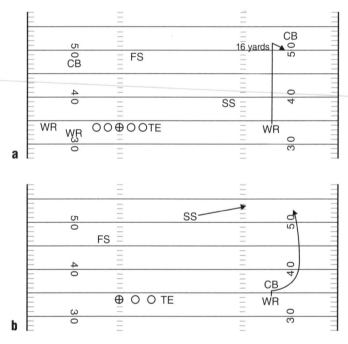

FIGURE 7.9 The 16-yard comeback: *(a)* The receiver turns outside and comes back toward the boundary; *(b)* the route converts versus rotation or Cover 2.

12-Yard Post Route

On a 12-yard post route (figure 7.10), the receiver uses vertical speed up the field. At 12 yards, he sticks his outside foot in the ground and runs to the near upright of the goalpost. He must be able to adjust to the defender. If the defender is playing high, the ball may be flattened off to the receiver and thrown short on a line. If the defender is shallow, the ball may be thrown high over the top and upfield. Either way, the receiver must be ready to adjust.

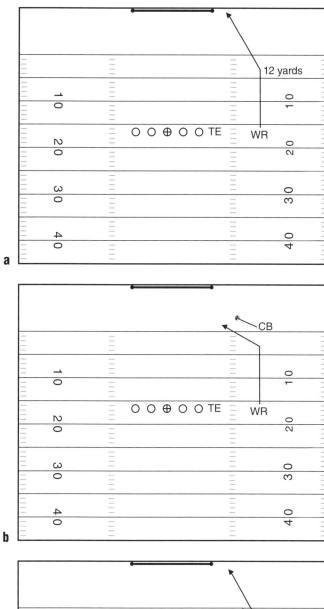

FIGURE 7.10 The 12-yard post route: *(a)* Receiver works to the near upright; *(b)* receiver flattens out versus a deep defender; *(c)* receiver goes deep versus a tight underneath defender.

Go Ball

On a go-ball route (figure 7.11), the receiver wants to run right at the defender. When the receiver gets close enough to step on the defender's toes, the receiver should explode past him and stay as tight to the defender's alignment as possible.

The key to running a great go ball is that the receiver must not allow the defender to run him to the boundary. As the receiver goes past the defender, he should hold his ground and try to get on top of the defender.

We never want the receiver to get any closer than 5 yards to the boundary so he has room to fade outside if the ball is thrown to the outside (figure 7.11*b*). We call this giving the quarterback some box outside. On all go balls versus press coverage, the receiver must beat the defender in the first 5 yards of the route and then hold the defender off as he works down the field.

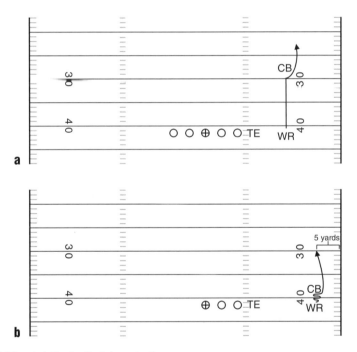

FIGURE 7.11 *(a)* Go ball; *(b)* go ball versus press coverage.

Fade Route

In the red zone, we like to throw to spots. The receiver and quarterback must be on the same page regarding where they are working to.

On the fade route (figure 7.12), the receiver wants to win at the line of scrimmage and explode to the back pylon. Under center, the quarterback takes one step from center and places the ball on the back pylon. He wants to put the ball back where nobody can make a play on it but the offensive player.

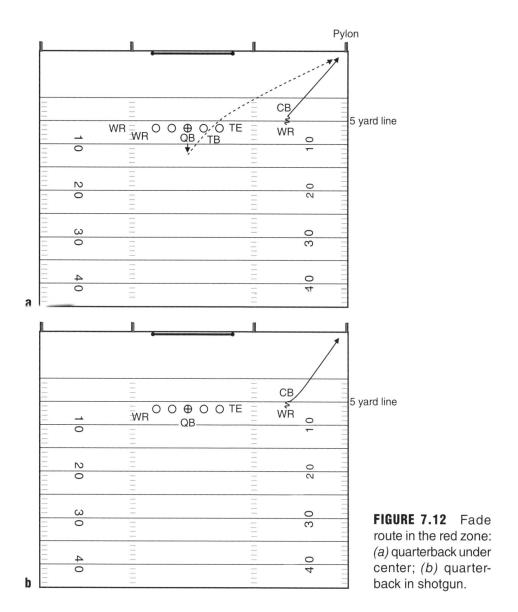

FIGURE 7.12   Fade route in the red zone: *(a)* quarterback under center; *(b)* quarterback in shotgun.

In the shotgun (figure 7.12*b*), the timing is a little slower. The quarterback gets the ball a split second later. The receiver works the route on the line of scrimmage for a moment before he runs to the back pylon.

The fade route is a great weapon in the red zone. It is the one pass that an offense can throw against almost any coverage if they have an accurate thrower and a receiver who will go get it. This is also a specific route that plays to personnel. If a team has a big rangy receiver who will go up and get the ball, the team definitely wants to use him in these situations. There is nothing like a big receiver with a great vertical reach who can really go up for the ball in the red zone. He will always be an offensive threat in this area of the field.

Tiny Diagonal Drill

SETUP: Wide receivers line up in single file. Eight cones are set up in a mini diagonal course with cones 4 to 5 inches apart (figure 7.13). This drill can be done off the field and should only take up about 4 to 5 yards. It's a good idea to do this drill off the main field so you don't chew up the grass.

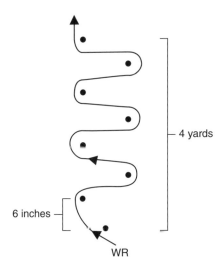

FIGURE 7.13 Tiny diagonal drill.

EXECUTION:

1. The first wide receiver in line foot fires around the cones, maintaining a good forward body lean.
2. The receiver's hands should pump as quickly as his feet, and the hands and feet should work in unison.
3. The wide receiver works through the course down and back.

COACHING POINTS: The tiny diagonal drill is a good one for teaching the wide receiver to move the hands and feet together, but it also works as a conditioning drill. This is a great warm-up drill to use at the beginning of the individual period.

High-Knee Plant Foot Drill

SETUP: Wide receivers line up in single file. Cones are set up about 3 feet apart in a diagonal course, a little wider than the diagonal course for the tiny diagonal drill.

EXECUTION:

1. Keeping the knees high, the wide receiver works through the zigzag course at about half speed.
2. When the wide receiver gets to a cone, he plants his foot (figure 7.14*a*) and changes direction toward the next diagonal cone (figure 7.14*b*).
3. This drill is not done at full speed because the wide receiver wants to get the feel of his body changing directions.
4. Pads should be over the plant foot on every break.

FIGURE 7.14 High-knee plant foot drill: *(a)* Receiver runs with high knees to the cone and plants his foot; *(b)* the receiver changes direction toward the next cone.

COACHING POINTS: Speed is not the emphasis of this drill. The emphasis is on using high knees and popping the plant foot on the break. The receiver should learn what it feels like to change his body position at the top of a route.

Four-Corner Cone Drill, Right-Angle Breaks

SETUP: Wide receivers stand in a single-file line. Cones are set about 4 feet apart in a square box. Do not make the box too big.

EXECUTION:

1. The receiver runs vertically to the first cone and plants his left, or outside, foot. The emphasis is on changing direction, not on how far the player has to run to get into his break.
2. The receiver must keep his pads over his feet on the break.
3. The receiver feels the plant and accelerates on the plant foot.
4. The receiver plants with the outside foot and pulls with the inside elbow. The hands and feet work together.
5. The receiver should feel the body and learn to control the change of direction.
6. The receiver plants and breaks right on the first three cones.
7. Off the third cone, the coach hits the receiver with a ball (figure 7.15).
8. On the second time through, the receiver reverses his path, planting with his right foot and breaking left on the first three cones. Off the third cone, the coach hits the receiver with a ball.

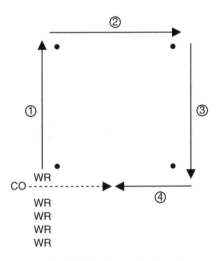

FIGURE 7.15   Four-corner cone drill, right-angle breaks.

COACHING POINTS: This is another route running drill that is not run at full speed. The receiver must be under control as he makes each break. He must learn how it feels when the body is in control as he plants and breaks on each cone.

Four-Corner Cone Drill, Diagonal Course

SETUP: Wide receivers stand in a single-file line. The cones are set up the same as in the four-corner cone drill with right-angle breaks. In this drill, players work diagonally through the course.

EXECUTION:

1. The receiver runs vertically to the first cone. When he reaches the first cone, he plants his left foot and turns right to run diagonally through the middle of the box to the far cone.

2. At the next cone, the receiver plants his right foot and turns left to run to the next cone.

3. At the next cone, the receiver plants his right foot and turns left to again run through the middle of the box.

4. Off the break at the third cone, the coach hits the receiver with a pass to finish the drill (figure 7.16).

5. On the second time through, the receiver reverses his route. At the first cone, he plants with his right foot and breaks left, runs diagonally through the box to the next cone, plants with his left foot and breaks right to run to the next cone, and plants with his left foot and breaks right, running diagonally through the box. The coach hits the receiver with a pass to finish the drill.

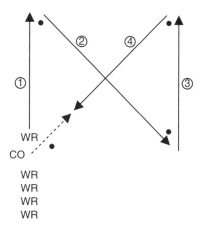

FIGURE 7.16   Four-corner cone drill, diagonal course.

COACHING POINTS: The key to this drill is to feel the body control off the plant. The player should come out of each break cleanly with no false steps. The shoulders should be over the plant foot on each break.

Man on Hip, Club by Him Drill

SETUP: Set up a box with cones about 8 yards apart. Wide receivers stand in two lines. The coach stands in the middle of the box.

EXECUTION:

1. Two players start the drill side by side. These two players go at the same time, working as partners.
2. The outside player is the wide receiver, and the inside player is the defensive back.
3. On the coach's command, the outside wide receiver strides upfield.
4. The defensive back stays right on his hip.
5. At the top of the break (where the cone is located), the wide receiver clubs by the defensive player and comes flat underneath on a dig route.
6. The receiver should focus on using vertical speed to get upfield and then dropping his weight and clubbing by the defender.

COACHING POINTS: Wide receivers must learn to identify the defender while running the route so they know how he is covering. Is he trailing or is he on the receiver's hip? The technique you use to get open will be determined by how the defender is playing you.

Out and Up Drill (Double Moves)

SETUP: Wide receivers stand in a single-file line. A cone is set up about 8 yards deep.

EXECUTION:

1. The first wide receiver comes off the ball vertically.
2. The receiver works upfield to a cone about 8 yards deep.
3. At the cone, the receiver drops his hips, plants his foot, and breaks out.
4. The receiver peeks back for a couple steps, plants the outside foot, and breaks back upfield.

COACHING POINTS: When making double moves, you need to cut down your strides so you can get in and out of breaks. A shortened stride will help you control your body to get in and out of short breaks.

Partner Trail Head-and-Shoulders Drill

SETUP: Wide receivers stand in two lines.

EXECUTION:

1. The wide receiver starts in front, and the defender works in a trail position directly behind the wide receiver as he goes upfield.

2. The wide receiver must identify where the defensive back is as he works upfield.

3. At the top of the break (with the defensive back in a trail position), the wide receiver gives the defensive back a head-and-shoulders fake to set up the defender and create separation. This simple head-and-shoulders fake often gives the wide receiver the step of separation he needs to get open on the route.

4. As the wide receiver comes out of the break, he comes as flat as possible and gets friendly on the ball. The receiver must be careful not to drift downfield away from the quarterback. (Getting friendly means always pressing back toward the quarterback so the receiver can beat the defensive back to the ball.)

COACHING POINTS: The previous two drills work on two situations that come up all the time in bump-and-run coverage. These are examples of having two specific tools in your tool kit. You need a tool for when the defender is on your hip at the break point, and you need a tool for when the man is in a trail technique. Just as there is a different application for a hammer and a screwdriver, you want to use different techniques versus different defensive coverage techniques. The key is to see the technique, recognize it, and quickly apply the proper tool in your tool kit to defeat the defender. That's why I always tell players that they have to develop several tools to be able to attack a variety of defensive techniques.

Top of a Curl Route

SETUP: Wide receivers stand in two lines; they will work as partners. The inside player is on offense, and the outside player is on defense. Both players start about 6 yards from a cone.

EXECUTION:

1. On the coach's command, the wide receiver heads upfield and runs the top of a curl route.

2. The wide receiver gets up the field to the break point with the pads over the toes; then he plants and comes back to the coach or the quarterback. The defender mirrors the receiver and tries to apply pressure on the receiver as he runs the route.

COACHING POINTS: The wide receiver can work the top of the route with the defensive back leaning on his body as they run up the field. The good thing about the drill is that it limits running. Players end up running only about 5 yards. This is good practice for separating versus tight coverage at the top of the route.

Routes on Air

SETUP: This drill is done with the quarterbacks. The quarterbacks are in the middle of the field. The receivers are right and left of the quarterbacks in their normal alignment.

EXECUTION:

1. The coach calls out the desired route to be run.
2. The receiver runs the desired route full speed at the desired depth.
3. The quarterback uses the proper footwork and delivers the ball on time to complete the route.

COACHING POINTS: Routes on air are used to practice the timing of all the routes with the quarterbacks. Usually, we start with the three-step game, slants, and hitches. Next, we go to the five-step game, outs, and curls. Then we work down the field to some of the deeper routes, including the digs and comebacks. We won't work every route every day in practice, but as we cycle through plays, we need to get repetitions on any throw that is a pattern in the offense. This also goes for any bootleg, naked, or sprint-out plays.

One-on-Ones

SETUP: The quarterbacks are in the middle of the field with a center or a manager snapping the football. The receivers are right and left. Receivers take repetitions one at a time. The defensive backs can play press man or off man.

EXECUTION:

1. The receiver and quarterback communicate the route that they want to work on each repetition. They should work every base route so the quarterback and receiver can gain confidence on each route.

2. The receiver should run every route full speed and should finish each catch with a 10- to 15-yard burst up the field. This just reinforces good practice habits.

COACHING POINTS: We like to call these one-on-ones. This is a time in practice when the wide receiver can work on his technique versus off and press man-to-man. This is when the quarterback and receiver really get to know how they will attack man coverage. The quarterback will see and experience how the wide receiver comes out of the break versus man coverage. Rotate between running routes in the field and running routes in the red zone and the tight zone inside the 12-yard line. Quarterbacks and receivers work on the timing of route running versus man-to-man coverage. The receiver also works on his hand fundamentals and subtle moves to gain the separation necessary to beat man coverage. This is a great period for working on route running skills and improving the timing between quarterbacks and receivers.

Split 'em Drill

SETUP: This drill is done out on the field. Receivers are in their normal alignment. Receivers work in a single-file line, one at a time. Two players in the back of the line need to step out in front of the drill and take a position 10 yards from the first receiver in line. These two receivers hold hand shields and simulate linebackers in underneath coverage.

EXECUTION:

1. On the coach's command, the receiver runs vertically and stops. The coach throws him the ball.
2. The receiver catches the ball, sticks his toe in the ground, and goes straight vertically (figure 7.17a). The player must go vertically.
3. The two players with hand shields converge on the receiver and hit him with the hand shields (figure 7.17b).
4. The receiver protects the ball and accelerates through contact (figure 7.17c). He continues to accelerate vertically upfield.

COACHING POINTS: This was one of Al Davis' favorite drills when I was with the Oakland Raiders. The emphasis is for every receiver who catches the ball underneath to immediately stick a foot in the ground and get vertical north and south. The ballcarrier must learn to get his pads down on contact, explode on contact, and protect the football.

FIGURE 7.17 Split 'em drill: (a) The receiver catches the ball and goes vertically; (b) the players with hand shields hit the receiver; (c) the receiver protects the ball and accelerates through the contact.

Summary

We have talked about the pure expression of route running. The skill of being a great route runner takes smarts and great body control as well as a detailed personality. It also takes a real understanding of how the defense will react to what you do to them. Overall, the skill of route running reflects on the player's agility as well as his understanding of how to attack the defense. In the next chapter, we will explore how to play well and help the team without the ball in your hands. The art of blocking is the topic of the next chapter.

8

Blocking

Good receivers play hard without the ball. Playing unselfishly is a big part of being a team player. A typical college football game has an average of 72 offensive plays. A good receiver will be lucky to get 8 to 10 passes thrown his way during the course of a game. That leaves 62 plays a game on which the wide receiver won't get the football. This chapter is about how the receiver can still be a team player and help his team win even when the ball doesn't come his way.

Playing with great effort when you don't get the ball is difficult, but the ways that you can help your team are immense. Blocking is not natural for a wide receiver, but it is essential for offensive success. Blocking depends mostly on an attitude that has to be developed. When a player gets it, his effort stands out and is inspiring to his offensive teammates.

Blocking is a base fundamental that you must learn in order to play the game of football. Games are won and lost on blocking and tackling. You can't truly love the game without appreciating a great block. Great wide receivers are more proud of the touchdown-springing blocks they make than the acrobatic catches.

Effort Areas for Wide Receivers

Consistently explode off the football on every snap. The defense should never be able to tell whether it's a run or pass by the way the receiver comes off the ball. A good receiver comes off the football with speed and acceleration every time, whether it's a run or a pass. If a player comes off at half speed on run plays, this makes the player and the offense very predictable for the defenders.

Get your man in the run game on every snap. On every running play, every offensive player is assigned to block a man. If everyone on offense makes his block and sustains it, the team should have a successful offensive play. The receiver usually has a corner or a safety on perimeter plays or a linebacker in the slot. The running back shouldn't have to worry about getting hit by that guy. As a receiver, you must have great pride in not letting the running back get hit by your defensive man.

Pile up wide receiver knockdowns. In every game, we have an offensive goal of getting 100 knockdowns. That goal has become more difficult with the changed cut rules in the 2011 season. The breakdown is 20 knockdowns for the receivers, 20 for tight ends, 20 for running backs, and 40 for the offensive line. This is a gauge for our offensive team on how physically we are playing. A knockdown is when an offensive player knocks his defender down on a play. An offensive player is also awarded a knockdown when he knocks a defensive back off the playing field or out of bounds. When the offense gets inside the 5-yard line and an offensive player blocks his man into the end zone, that is also a knockdown. We have one more way that a skill guy can get a knockdown. An offensive skill player can get a knockdown by making a defender miss when the offensive player has the ball in his hands. Every defender whom a ballcarrier makes miss is a knockdown for the offense. Players will have equal opportunities to get knockdowns on run and pass plays. Things don't happen on a football field by accident. Things happen because of intent. Offensive players have to be intentional about wanting to get knockdowns in any way they can.

Gain yards after the catch (YAC). Come alive with the ball in your hands! When the ball is in the air, the receiver wants to catch the ball, clutch it and put it away, and then come alive as a ballcarrier. Great wide receivers have the ability to make people miss in the open field. You have to practice making big plays in practice. When you catch the ball in practice, take it and run for a good 15 yards after the catch. When I was with the Oakland Raiders, we had Jerry Rice. When he caught the ball in practice, he used to score almost every time. He would catch a 5-yard pass, weave through the defense, and sprint another 60 yards to the end zone. We want to see a 15-yard sprint after every catch in practice. On Full-Finish Thursday, every ball caught goes to the house. It is something to see when guys score on every play! There's nothing like seeing a guy get another gear when the ball is in his hands and blow the doors off the defense.

Make big-play blocks! The more I observe the great players, the more I'm convinced that great players work harder to do the little things better than anyone else. That's what makes them great. Simple hard work making your block or hustling downfield to get on your man will create big-play blocks. There is nothing more unselfish than a receiver hustling from the backside to make the last big block to spring a ballcarrier for a touchdown downfield.

Go for double knockdowns (extra-effort blocks). A knockdown is great, but a double knockdown is even better. For a double knockdown, a player gets a knockdown then gets up and, instead of being satisfied, keeps playing and gets another knockdown on the same play. We have clips of guys getting three knockdown blocks on one play. That's just playing as hard as you can to the whistle.

Make big hits on crack blocks. In some of our perimeter schemes, the receiver short motions down and cracks the end man on the line of scrimmage. Then we pitch the ball on the outside on the perimeter. A crack block on the outside can really create a big running lane for the back, and getting a big hit from a receiver can excite an offense.

Contribute to the special-teams effort. We tell receivers that they are football players first. That means we expect them to help on special teams. Great receivers can be great special-teams players as well. I love players who can return kickoffs or punts. I love recruiting players who can run the ball in open space. Our best receivers over the years were also some of our best cover guys on punts and kickoffs. Good athletes can do whatever the team needs them to do on a football field. When I recruit, I always look for guys who are multidimensional, guys who can do a lot of things well. They will always be able to help the football team in some way. Athletes who have great agility and quickness and are physical and aggressive can do a lot for a football team on offense, defense, and special teams.

Blocking on the Perimeter

Blocking on the perimeter is 90 percent want-to. Many players are moved to the position of wide receiver when they are young because they don't have the defensive mentality of some of their teammates. Coaches often take young skill players who are physical and aggressive and play them on defense. Then they take the skill players who are not as physically aggressive and put them at receiver. That doesn't bother me. What does bother me is when I hear some youth coach say that you don't have to be physical if you are a wide receiver. Or I've heard some coaches say that they don't really care if the wide receivers are good blockers. In my world, nothing could be further from the truth.

"I try to be the most complete receiver I can be. Blocking is just want-to!"

Hines Ward, all-pro wide receiver for the Pittsburgh Steelers

Football is a team game. All offensive players should learn to block. For an offense to be effective, the team must be able to run the ball effectively. The offensive line has to do a great job of blocking in order for the run game to be effective. In our philosophy, the offensive line must block the defensive down linemen and ensure that the ball gets back to the line of scrimmage. The linebackers will be handled by the combinations up front with the offensive line and the tight ends. When the ball is run outside of the tight end, the wide receivers must do a great job or the play will be dead. On an outside run, the wide receivers' blocks must be an extension of the offensive line's blocks.

A wide receiver's ability to block on the perimeter comes down to body position, point of aim, and hustle. If you stay after it longer than the guys on the other side of the ball, you will be a good blocker as a receiver.

> **"I know when I go across the middle, nobody's going to let up on me or tackle me softly. They're going to try to knock my head off! That's the approach I try to take to the game. I'm going to go out there, and if I get an opportunity to hit and block you, I'm going to do it."**
>
> *Hines Ward, all-pro wide receiver for the Pittsburgh Steelers*

Stay between the ball and your man (figure 8.1). The receiver's job is simple but not easy. All the receiver has to do on any given run play is stay between his man and the football. Don't let your man make the tackle; it is really that simple. If you get your body in a good football position, stay in front of your man until the play is over, and don't let him make that tackle, you will be a great blocker on the perimeter.

FIGURE 8.1 When blocking on the perimeter, the receiver must stay between the ball and the defender he is blocking.

Blocking Downfield

Big runs are sprung by the wide receivers' blocks downfield. In the run game, the offensive line can often spring the running back for a nice gain into the secondary. But for the ball to go the distance, a wide receiver has to make a big block on a secondary player to get the running back into the end zone. The defensive secondary is the last line of defense. On a long play, the running back will often have just one man to beat in order to score. If the receivers are hustling and can make that circle block (figure 8.2), the running back may have a chance to score. Sometimes that is a one-on-one block straight ahead. Sometimes it's a hustling cross-field block on the deep safety who is trying to run the back down from the backside of the play. Often it comes down to who is playing the hardest and who wants it more—the defensive back or the wide receiver.

FIGURE 8.2   Receivers making a circle block on a defender downfield to give the running back a chance to score.

Fundamentals of Blocking

Blocking fundamentals are the same for every position. The great thing about blocking is that many of the techniques don't change regardless of position. I have learned all my techniques and fundamentals of blocking from the great line coaches I have been around, such as Bill Callahan and

Howard Mudd. Because receivers must learn to play and block in space, some differences exist in the blocking techniques used by receivers; however, the base fundamentals of blocking a man over you and controlling him and moving him are the same.

Football Position

The first thing I was taught about football when I was a kid was how to get in football position. When they taught us grass drills, the first thing we learned was the breakdown position (figure 8.3). The breakdown position is when your feet are about shoulder-width apart. Your weight is on the balls of your feet. You are bent at the waist, and your shoulders are over your toes. Your feet are buzzing up and down, and your hands are doing the same. This is the universal position in sports. It doesn't matter what game you are playing; you can change directions and move athletically if you are in this breakdown position. It is the fundamental movement position. If you play basketball, you will assume this same position when you play defense. If you play baseball, you'll assume this same position when getting ready to field a ground ball. You have to bend to get your body in position to play ball.

FIGURE 8.3 Breakdown position: feet shoulder-width apart, weight on balls of feet, bent at waist, shoulders over toes, feet and hands moving up and down. (a) Front view; (b) side view.

Leverage

Leverage is the most important thing that a player must understand in order to be a good and consistent blocker. Once a player truly understands body leverage, he can be an effective blocker no matter what size he is. Size doesn't matter in blocking. Body position, leverage, and desire are more important. Let's look at the key components to leverage.

The first key to leverage is getting a low base (figure 8.4). You should have wide feet on contact. Your feet should be wider than shoulder width on contact. A wide base gives you strength and a great foundation. A narrow base is bad because you will lack strength and can easily get thrown to the side and knocked off balance.

Another key to leverage is working pad under pad (figure 8.5). When two players are pushing on each other, the low man will have more power and control. Always work pad under pad and always work to be the low man.

FIGURE 8.4 Low base and wide feet on contact.

FIGURE 8.5 Pad under pad.

The next key component of leverage is hand placement. When blocking, you always want to work the hands inside (figure 8.6). The player who gets his hands inside will gain control. At the same time that you are working your hands inside, you should keep your elbows in and your thumbs to the sky. Keeping your elbows in and your thumbs to the sky will naturally keep your head back and give you more balance. When making contact on a block, many players make the mistake of letting their elbows go out; as a result, their head gets overextended, and they may fall forward. Keeping the thumbs to the sky keeps the elbows in and helps keep the blocker from getting overextended.

The next important point of leverage is the feet. You need to get the feet in the ground (figure 8.7). When getting the feet into the ground, you

FIGURE 8.6   Hands inside, elbows in, and thumbs to the sky.

FIGURE 8.7   Feet in the ground; flat-footed, short, choppy steps.

should get the foot as flat as possible with the toes pointing slightly out. You want to get as much of the foot on the ground as possible, with weight on the instep. You do not want to be on the toes. When working the feet with the weight on the insteps, you need to take short, choppy steps. Get the feet into the ground as many times as possible. Don't take long steps. Long steps will cause you to have only one foot on the ground for extended periods of time. Take short, choppy steps so you can get a lot of steps into the ground faster than your opponent.

In most blocking movements, there is a point of stalemate. At that point, you need to drive your hips toward the defender for power (figure 8.8). As you struggle for position and movement, keep trying to refit your hands to get control inside. Remember, the low man wins, the man who gets pad under pad wins, and the man with his hands inside gains control.

FIGURE 8.8   At the point of stalemate, the blocker drives his hips toward the defender.

Keys to Good Leverage

- Maintain a wide base.
- Get your pad under the defender's pad.
- Work your hands inside.
- Keep your elbows in and thumbs to the sky.
- Shift your weight to your insteps.
- Take short, choppy steps with the weight on the insteps of the feet.
- Drive your hips toward the defender for movement.
- Refit the hands inside.

Oklahoma Drill

The Oklahoma drill is probably the most famous drill in football. It was developed at Oklahoma by legendary Oklahoma coach Bud Wilkinson. This simple, fundamental drill is the essence of blocking and the basis for the game of football.

SETUP: The Oklahoma drill can be set up in a few different ways. In its base form, the drill includes an offensive man, a defensive man, and a ballcarrier. Set up two dummies about 4 yards apart on the ground for the ballcarrier to run between. This is a full-contact padded drill.

EXECUTION:

1. The offensive player and defensive player stand about 1 yard apart in a three-point stance. A tailback with a ball lines up 5 yards deep behind the offensive player.

2. On the snap, the offensive player and defensive player come off at one another.

3. The offensive player tries to block and move the defensive player out of the hole.

4. The defensive player tries to hit and shed the offensive player and then tackle the tailback, who is running through the hole.

5. Both the offensive player and the defensive player work on leverage techniques until one of them gains the advantage.

VARIATION: You can also do this drill without a ballcarrier. Gather up the team and have two players come off on one another and try to whip each other with technique.

COACHING POINTS: There is no secret to this drill. It's one of the best drills in football and has been around a long time because it works. For many coaches across America, this is the first drill they do on the first day that their team is in pads during training camp. By filming this drill, the coach can provide some of the greatest technique teaching of the entire year because the drill really emphasizes body positioning and leverage. Players should focus on getting hands inside and refitting, working pad under pad, and driving the hips through the block.

Oklahoma Three-on-Three

SETUP: This drill is similar to the previous drill but is done with three offensive blockers, three defensive players, and one running back. This time the goal is for the running back to gain 10 yards in three tries. Set up cones about 7 yards wide and make the course 10 yards long.

EXECUTION:

1. The offensive players get three downs to gain 10 yards.
2. If the defense holds them up in three tries, the defense wins.
3. If the offense gains 10 yards at any time in those three consecutive plays, the offense wins.
4. This is a great competitive drill for training camp, especially for teaching leverage. We give every position—offensive line, tight ends, and receivers—a shot at the drill.

COACHING POINTS: Make sure that neither team jumps offside in the drill. Holding calls also apply. Players must be responsible for playing with good technique. Players can learn to use the proper base, hand placement, and leverage from this drill, especially if the drill is filmed.

Stalk Blocking

Stalk blocking is a challenging skill because wide receivers work in space away from the formation. The stalk block has to be performed in a lot of green grass, which means the wide receiver has to be under control. If a wide receiver is out of control, he will surely miss the defender and have no chance of blocking him in space. The wide receiver also needs to understand the angle of the play and the defender's responsibility. Most corners are the contain players for the defense, so if the blocker attacks their outside number, they will widen and contain. This is very important on outside plays, especially for the receiver who is blocking on the perimeter.

Point of Attack

The point of attack is the spot on the defender's body that the wide receiver is attacking. For every specific run play, the receiver has a specific point of attack. For us, all inside runs (runs that go inside the tackles) call for an inside point of attack on the defensive back. For inside runs, the wide receiver blocks the defensive back on his inside number (figure 8.9). We are very specific on this landmark because we want the wide receiver to break down and get his body on this landmark before he engages the block.

On all outside plays, which go outside the tackle box, the receiver should use an outside aiming point. For us, an outside aiming point is the defender's outside number (figure 8.10). Of course, if the defender doesn't

FIGURE 8.9 For an inside run, the wide receiver blocks the defensive back on his inside number.

FIGURE 8.10 For an outside run, the wide receiver blocks the defensive back on his outside number.

have an outside number, the receiver can just imagine where that outside number would be. The receiver must be specific here because we want him to break down 2 yards from that point of aim on every outside play. If the wide receiver breaks down on the outside number, he should get a specific reaction from the defender. Most defenders are taught to keep their outside arm and leg free. Simply by breaking down on the defender's outside number, the wide receiver can get the defender to widen, and this creates space for the running back.

Work to Stay Square

Remember, the whole idea of blocking is to cover up your man and create running lanes for the running back. In trying to create running lanes for the running back, a receiver needs to fight to stay square on all blocks. We tell the perimeter blockers that if the defender moves, they should try to slide like a basketball player and stay directly on their landmark. This should be easy if the blocker's focus stays on that landmark. When the wide receiver is sliding, he should work to stay as square as possible to the line of scrimmage. We say that the running back should always be able to read the back of the receiver's jersey (figure 8.11). When the wide receiver fights to stay square, he forces the defensive back to widen and run around the block. By staying square, the wide receiver creates a bigger running lane or alley for the back.

FIGURE 8.11   When the receiver is staying square to his defender, the running back should be able to read the back of his jersey.

Contact

Once the blocker gets engaged, he should stay engaged and run his feet. Once he makes contact with the defensive back, the blocker should not let him off. When the defender tries to release and run to the ball, the blocker should run his feet, keep his body on the defender, and finish the block. All blockers must learn to run their feet on contact because the defender is not going to just stop on contact; the defender will try to release and run to the ball. Running your feet on contact is the key to finishing every block, especially when blocking in space.

"Whoever plays the hardest for the longest, wins!"

NFL offensive coordinator Tom Moore

Keys to Stalk Blocking

- Identify your point of aim. The point of aim you choose will depend on the type of running play. The point of attack should be a specific point on the uniform—the inside or outside number.
- Break down 2 yards from the defender.
- Stay in good football position and make the defender come through you to the football.
- React to the defensive back's charge by sliding your body laterally.
- Stay in a good football stance and engage the defender with your eyes and hands right on the point of attack.
- Lead with your hands. Work them inside the defender's hands.
- Work to stay as square to the line of scrimmage as possible.
- Engage to get into a fitted position of leverage. Once you get engaged, stay engaged.
- Keep your feet alive and run on contact.
- Fight to keep your body between the defender and the ball.
- Finish the block and fight to stay as square to the line of scrimmage as possible.

Leverage Drill

SETUP: An offensive player and a defensive player line up chest to chest on the sideline. Both players should lock up as if they are pushing against each other.

EXECUTION:

1. On the coach's command "hit," the offensive man gets low in a fitted position on the defender and works all his leverage points (figure 8.12). Both players should have wide feet on contact.

2. The offensive player foot fires with small steps on his insteps. He keeps fitting the hands inside. He works the defender to the numbers as the defensive player provides resistance.

3. Once the players get to the numbers, the coach yells "switch." The defender becomes the offensive player, and he works all his leverage skills on the other player against that player's resistance.

4. The two players work back to the sideline to finish the drill.

COACHING POINTS: This drill emphasizes the key elements of leverage: Focus on low pads. Keep the hands inside with the thumbs pointing to the sky. Stay in a wide base and on your insteps. Refit your hands to get them back inside and in the best blocking position. This is a great drill for learning leverage and blocking position.

FIGURE 8.12 Leverage drill.

Mirror Dodge at Half Speed for Body Position

SETUP: This drill is done with two players; one player is on offense, and the other is on defense. The defensive player indicates the movement in the drill. This is a half-speed drill that enables players to work on body positioning. Set up two cones 4 yards apart.

EXECUTION:

1. The offensive player starts in a good football position.
2. The defensive player slides to each cone (the cones are set 4 yards apart).
3. Just like in basketball, the wide receiver slides to keep his body directly in front of the defender (figure 8.13a).
4. When the defender gets to the cone, he pauses for a second, and the offensive player engages him with his hands (figure 8.13b).
5. Then the defensive player works across to the next cone, pauses, and engages.
6. Both players work this movement three times, staying down in a good body position.
7. Each player should get a chance to be on offense.

COACHING POINTS: This is a half-speed drill. The total emphasis is on body position. Before a receiver can execute a block, he must first get his body in position to block. The key is to stay in a good football position with bent knees and to stay in front of the defender, just like a basketball player playing slide defense.

FIGURE 8.13 Mirror dodge at half speed for body position: *(a)* Receiver slides to mirror the defender between the cones; *(b)* at the cone, the defender pauses, and the receiver engages him with his hands.

Mirror Dodge at Full Speed

SETUP: This is a competitive drill with an offensive player and a defensive player. The defensive man is the rabbit. Set up two cones 4 yards apart.

EXECUTION:

1. The rabbit's job is to try to change directions and run around either of the two cones three times.

2. The rabbit can use spin moves, head-and-shoulder fakes, changes of direction, or any other move that he wants.

3. The offensive player's job is to slide between the cones, not giving up any ground, and keep the rabbit from running around the cones.

4. The offensive player should stay square.

5. The defensive player, the rabbit, should work on one side of the cones.

6. The offensive player should also get engaged and stay engaged. Once he gets his hands on the defensive back, he should not let him off. The offensive player should run his feet and keep his body on the defender.

7. The rabbit tries to run around the cones three times. If he is successful, the offensive player does 20 fingertip push-ups. If the offensive player is able to keep the defender out, the defender does 20 fingertip push-ups. This extra motivation helps make the drill more realistic and gamelike.

COACHING POINTS: This is a great drill because it is really competitive. The emphasis should be on learning great body position. The drill forces the wide receiver to be tenacious and to keep coming after the defender.

Stalk and Run on an Outside Target

SETUP: This drill simulates an outside running play. Two receivers—one on offense, one on defense—work as partners. The defensive player is 5 to 6 yards off the line of scrimmage. A manager or another receiver acts as a tailback in the backfield.

EXECUTION:

1. On the snap, the coach hands the ball off to the tailback, who runs all the way outside the receiver's block on a wide outside course.

2. The receiver comes off the ball and breaks down square on the outside number of the defensive back.

3. The defensive player engages the receiver. As the tailback breaks contain, the defensive player should fight to keep his outside arm and leg free and run to the outside to contain the ball.

4. The receiver should engage the defender and run to his outside number. He continues to try to reach the outside number all the way to the sideline.

COACHING POINTS: The key to this perimeter block on an outside run play is that the receiver must break down and put his nose on the defender's outside number. As the defender continues to widen, the receiver needs to stay square and run his feet to stay on that outside landmark. As he makes this block, the receiver should stay as square as he can. The key coaching point is that the back running the ball should be able to read the back of the receiver's jersey. This way the running back will be able to choose where to run the ball—inside or outside the receiver's block. The common mistake that receivers make is just turning out to block the defender when the defender moves outside. This will only give the back one choice on his cut.

Running Cut and Crab

SETUP: Receivers stand in two lines. Two coaches, or a coach and a manager, each hold a square dummy. The dummies are about 5 to 7 yards from the receivers. The coaches hold the dummies off to the side, holding them with one hand by the handle.

EXECUTION:

1. Players get one repetition with the right shoulder and one repetition with the left shoulder.

2. On the cadence, both receivers at the front of the lines run and dip and cut through the dummies.

3. For the right shoulder, the receiver dips and balls the right hand like a fist. He draws back that fist and throws it at the dummy, punching the dummy on the lower half, He runs and extends through the dummy.

4. On contact, the receiver rolls through the dummy.

5. The receiver hits the ground and rolls, popping up on all fours to crab walk for another 10 yards. He finishes through the line.

6. The receiver repeats the drill, hitting with the left shoulder coming back.

COACHING POINTS: Cut blocking is a skill that must be mastered. When making this block on a live player in a game, the receiver should throw the fist right through the defender's crotch. The head and shoulder work to hit the thigh. Emphasis is placed on cutting and running through the defender; the receiver should not just extend and dive on the ground. A cut block is a highly effective block when a defender is running hard at you and is trying to run you over (and is not protecting his legs). When players learn how to read a defender's body language, this can be a really effective block.

Summary

Blocking is the very essence of football. The first thing a player must learn is to get his body in position to block. Once he has done that many times, he doesn't even have to think to get the job done. Just getting the body in position is half the battle. Great receivers are proud of their big plays, but I have to admit that they giggle like little kids when they get a big block. They wear it like a badge of honor. Just like everything a receiver does, the receiver's blocks are on the perimeter for everyone to see, whether good or bad. Often these blocks spring runners for touchdowns. For a receiver to be truly complete, he must take great pride in this area of his game. Being a good blocker is all about playing hard. In the next chapter, we will take a hard look at playing smart.

9
Playing Smart

Ted Williams was the last hitter in Major League Baseball to hit over .400 in a season. He did it with great physical skill and also a great mental approach to hitting a baseball. Ted Williams had three rules of hitting. Rule 1: Always get a good pitch to hit. A good batter should never swing at a bad pitch, because it limits the batter's ability to hit the ball hard. Rule 2: Always take proper thinking to the plate. You have to have done your homework. What is this pitcher's best pitch? What did he get you out on last time? The answers to these questions give you the information you need for success. Rule 3: Be quick with the bat.

Williams' second rule—take proper thinking to the plate—applies to all sports, including football. Some of the greatest coaches talk about the importance of the mental approach and playing smart. This will help your winning formula as a player.

"God gets you to the plate, but once you're there, you are on your own."

Ted Williams, hall of fame player for the Boston Red Sox

I am a student of great coaches. One of my favorite teachers and coaches is Bob Knight, the great Indiana basketball coach. In his autobiography *Knight: My Story*, he devotes an entire chapter to the cornerstones that formed him as a coach. I often refer to his thoughts when making points to our players about their mental approach to the game. At Ohio State, Bob Knight played for a great coach named Fred Taylor. Knight said Taylor had an unyielding, untiring passion for teaching kids to understand basketball and carry this understanding and commitment into life. This is the greatest reminder for me, because I have dedicated my life to coaching and teaching kids. This is what great coaches do; they have an unyielding desire to teach constantly. They are always trying to have their players understand more.

Coaches teach and conduct practice for weeks or sometimes even months before they get to a competitive game. A coach's ultimate goal is to send a player onto the field as a free-thinking individual who is self-sufficient and has the ability, knowledge, and mental and physical tools to handle any situation. Coaches hope players have the necessary experiences that produce confidence on the field during competition.

"All my life, I've had six honest serving men.
They taught me all I knew.
Their names were what, where, and when;
how, why, and who."

Bob Knight in Knight: My Story

Ask Questions

Learn to ask the right questions. As we become older and more experienced in life, we learn to ask more questions. Experience tells us that the more information we have before making a decision, the better our chances of making the right and proper decision. Information is power. It is the same in sports. Players need to learn to take in all the information they can so they make the best decisions on the field.

As a player elevates to high school, college, and the professional level, his preparation becomes key to his performance. The player must ask the right questions. Who is starting at right corner? How long has he been the starter? How does he like to play man coverage? Is he very fast? Is he a good tackler? Does he like to play physically? What type of defense does this team like to play? Do they like to blitz? Do they do anything to tip off their blitzes? What type of body language tips do they show when they are going to blitz or play man? Players must learn to ask questions so they can gather the information they need to make winning decisions on the field. The key is to get players to play intelligently. Players should not only understand a skill or technique, but should also know why it works.

Great players maximize their talents and make everyone around them better. They understand the game and their own strengths and weaknesses as well as the strengths and weaknesses of their opponents and teammates. They learn this process by thinking.

Play the Percentages

Playing smart is playing the percentages. Playing smart is the most elementary piece of success in all of sports. It is also one of the least talked about. I believe that more players are coming into college football without the ability to really think about the game. The ability to see and gather critical information—and the ability to use it to your advantage and play the percentages—is the essence of playing smart. Players have different degrees of this ability, but the really smart ones separate themselves as game changers. Derek Jeter, Michael Jordan, Larry Bird, Kobe Bryant, and Tom Brady are great players who are known for playing with their heads. These players learned to take information and use it for competitive advantage for their team.

> **"Fortunate, indeed, is the man who takes exactly the right measure of himself."**
>
> *Peter Mere Latham*

You must understand your own strengths and weaknesses. Before a player can understand his opponent's strengths and weaknesses, he must understand his own. Coaches spend a lot of time getting to know the strengths and weaknesses of all their players. A player needs to know what he can do, but he must equally understand what he cannot do.

As Clint Eastwood said in *The Outlaw Josey Wales*, "A man's got to know his limitations." Great players know what they can and cannot do to be effective on the field. Some wide receivers are short and quick. They rely on their elusiveness to be effective. Some wide receivers are big and strong. They learn to body up on people when they get in one-on-one situations.

Great players are realistic about their abilities. A player's greatest asset may be that he realistically knows what he can and cannot do. In the heat of battle, he can make the right choices about what to try and what not to try. A great player must utilize his strengths, and maybe more important, he must minimize his weaknesses to the best of his ability so they don't hurt his overall performance. Playing smart is a function of playing the percentages. It is a function of position, placement, and recognition. Playing smart is a key to winning in all sports.

Understand Wins and Losses

Understanding is so important. Players have to understand why teams lose and why players fail. Teams lose because they turn the ball over on offense. Teams lose because they give up big plays on defense. Teams lose because they commit foolish penalties. Teams lose because they get outhit as a team and they aren't physical enough. Teams lose because of too many mental errors—they make more mistakes than their opponents. There's an old saying that before you can win, you must learn to stop losing.

> **"Dumb loses more than smart wins."**
>
> *Bob Knight when asked about another team's NCAA loss*

Many coaches think that more games are lost than are won. It's difficult to argue with this idea. When two teams are competing hard, physical mistakes will sometimes happen. As much as you don't want them to happen and you work diligently to prevent them from happening, sometimes they do, and that is often just part of the ups and downs of the game.

Those types of mistakes don't bother coaches as much as the foolish mental mistakes that we all work so hard to avoid. A foolish mental mistake is running the wrong route on a play. A foolish penalty is jumping offside or lining up in an illegal formation. These are examples of foolish mistakes that get teams beat. These are the types of errors that drive coaches crazy because if players are focused and mentally in tune with what they are doing, these mistakes can and should be avoided. We have all seen a team or a player make a critical unforced mistake that cost the game. When coaches take over a team that has been losing for a long time, they often say that the team must first learn to stop beating themselves before they can learn how to win.

Why Teams Lose

- Foolish mental errors
- Turnovers
- Foolish penalties
- Poor effort
- Poor recognition and awareness
- Poor preparation
- Poor communication
- Giving up minus-yardage plays
- Being outhit as a team by not being physical

Concentrate

Concentration is a special quality in sports. I have coached at both the professional and college levels. The single quality that keeps most rookie players from having a chance to play well their first year is the ability to concentrate. Success is difficult for a freshman in college or a rookie in his first year in the NFL for many reasons. One reason is that there is so much information for them to digest and understand their first season. Players must learn all the plays and know their exact assignments on every new play. Players must play in stadiums and places they are not familiar with. They have new teammates whom they are still getting to know. All these experiences are new to the player. Plus, the player is competing against players who are faster, stronger, and more athletic (not to mention more experienced) than he is used to competing against. To take in all this information and feel comfortable—to be able to master it and then zero in and concentrate on doing a great job—is a challenge for most young players. Mistakes will happen along the way. Concentration usually comes from experience. Sometimes players have to learn from their mistakes in order to experience this level of concentration.

Learn to Concentrate

- Concentration starts with looking and seeing. In football, everyone looks but not everyone sees the situation.
- Concentration starts with hearing and listening. Most people hear, but few really listen.
- Good concentration leads to anticipation, recognition, reaction, and execution.

The 1985 Chicago Bears were recently voted one of the greatest teams in NFL history. After college, I was lucky enough to spend close to two seasons with the Chicago Bears in 1987 and 1988. It was an exciting time for the Bears, just coming off a world championship. The Chicago roster was filled with characters and future hall of fame players. The great Walter Payton was finishing his career, and Mike Ditka was the coach. One of the players who fascinated me was middle linebacker Mike Singletary. Singletary was one of the most feared and respected middle linebackers in the NFL. They used to call him "Samurai Mike" after the *Saturday Night Live* character John Belushi played, who used to scream at the top of his lungs and cut up sandwiches with a samurai sword. Mike was a passionate and intense player and was extremely smart. I was a journeyman player just trying to make the roster, but the time I spent in Chicago had a real impact on me and my life in football.

One day in training camp, we were in a full-padded team session. The offense broke the huddle. As the quarterback got under center, Mike Singletary started calling out the play: "Here they come, baby, it's an I-so right here! They are going to run an I-so right here!" The rookie fullback came out of the huddle and stared down his blocking assignment as he got down in his alignment. Then Singletary let out this primal shriek that sent chills down everyone's spine. You could see that rookie fullback just melt in his stance. When the ball was snapped, Singletary hit the fullback in the backfield like a freight train almost before he could get out of his stance. Half the defense was there a split second later. The screams and shrieks continued. Singletary had called out the play before it even happened. He saw the formation and read the eyes of the fullback coming out of the huddle. He may have seen that the offensive linemen were heavy in their stances, which was another tip-off for run. He used all that critical information to diagnose the play before it happened. That rookie fullback learned a valuable lesson from a hall of famer that day. So did I.

That story is an example of how a veteran player such as Singletary used every little piece of critical information to diagnose the situation. His knowledge of playing smart gave him an edge as a player. It's another example of how the great players do the little things better than the rest.

Prepare

Preparation is the process of thinking about what you will do if something happens. I have been around some great experienced players who really knew the game inside and out. I spent four years with the Indianapolis Colts. Peyton Manning was masterful at using a dummy cadence. A dummy cadence is how the quarterback uses the snap count to keep the defense off balance. To make the defense jump, Peyton would start his snap count as if he was going to snap the ball. Then, after the defense showed their alignment, he would call the best play to attack the defense. He wanted to use all the presnap information he could to gain an advantage on the defense. In sports, just like in life, information is power. Peyton was masterful in his preparation. His nickname was the Caveman because he would spend so much time watching film. Peyton had a reputation for taking impeccable notes, and as the week wound down, he would ask any and all questions until he felt totally prepared. He would write it all down in his notebook. He would keep files of his notes on players and coaches for future games; this was all part of his preparation so he could make the best and most educated decisions on game day.

Play Situational Football

A football game is made up of many different situations. Coaches spend a lot of time in practice talking about and working on these situations. At the college and professional levels, the practice week is broken down into specific work on these different situations. This includes first-and-10 situations in which the offense will work on certain plays. From there, the offense and defense get more specific and work on a variety of third-down plays. We work on specific things for third-and-long (10 yards or more) situations. We have other plays that we use for third and medium (4 to 6 yards). And we have an entirely different package that we use in third and short when we need only 1 yard.

Offensively, we may put more receivers on the field on third and long. On third and 1, we may bring in more tight ends and get into a heavier run formation because we need only 1 yard. As an offense, we expect different things from the defense in third and long than we do in third and short. That's where players have to be in tune to great situational football. They have to know what to expect in those different situations both offensively and defensively.

Third-Down Defenses

As players get more experience, they come to understand that the defense will respond a certain way on most down and distances. On third and long, the defense will usually play coverage and make the offense throw a short pass; the defense wants to come up and make the tackle, forcing the offense to punt. In this situation, the offense will typically see the defense using a more blanket coverage that is deeper and softer. In third and medium, the offense will see a different personality from the defense. The defense is more likely to blitz in this situation. Because of the down and distance, the defense will use tighter coverage and blitzes in a third-and-medium situation.

Red Zone

A red-zone situation refers to the offense entering the area from the +25-yard line to the 12-yard line on the opponent's end of the field. This area is also considered the scoring zone. The offense is in scoring position, so they never want to have a penalty or minus-yardage play in this situation. We have certain passes that we like to use from different distances in the red zone. Typically, we throw to spots down here. Most red-zone pass defenses don't protect the back corners of the end zone or the front pylons, so in our red-zone passes, we try to attack those areas that we think are left vulnerable by the defense. The coverage doesn't typically back up in the red zone because the defense has less field to cover. So receivers need to be ready to catch hard-thrown balls that are thrown through zones and put to the back of the endline. These are specific throws that we spend a lot of time working on over the course of the season.

Two-Minute Situation

The two-minute drill is another situation that comes up on a regular basis. These situations may arise at the end of a half or at the end of a game. The team may need a touchdown or a field goal at the end of the game to tie the game or win. We have a specific set of runs and passes that we use in the two-minute situation. Players must know how many time-outs the team has and how the team can stop the clock if it needs to. Receivers must know that when they catch the ball, they need to get all the yardage they can and then get out of bounds. The clock also stops on all incomplete passes. In college ball, the clock also stops when the offense gets a first down (until the chains are reset). In professional football, the clock continues to run when the offense gets a first down. Everyone must be locked into the rules in this specific situation; being aware of the rules could mean the difference between winning or losing a close game.

> **"Habit gives strength to the body in great exertion, to the mind in great danger, and to judgment against first impression."**
>
> *Carl von Clausewitz, the director of the General War Academy, Prussia*

Playing smart in situational football is what separates the best teams from the average ones. It is those critical situations that make up the difference between winning and losing. Bill Belichick, whose New England Patriots teams have been called some of the smartest teams in recent football history, attributes the team's success in winning three Super Bowls in four years to playing smart in situational football. He said, "The thing that has helped us win a lot of games is the players' ability to execute and perform in critical situations."

Summary

As a coach, I love the topic of playing smart. Many coaches were overachievers as players. They had to use every little advantage to get an edge. I was one of those guys. I can relate to finding any way to get an edge over your opponent. The guys who are the best at this are veteran NFL players. They are the survivors in the most competitive professional league. These veteran players have learned all the tricks over the years and have learned to use them well. When I coached for the Oakland Raiders in 2002 and 2003, we had an entire roster of amazing, crafty veteran players who combined had decades and decades of NFL knowledge. Guys such as Rich Gannon, Jerry Rice, Tim Brown, Lincoln Kennedy, Rod Woodson, and Bill Romanowski, just to name a few. These guys had a wealth of knowledge and, for the most part, were the epitome of playing smart. Not only were these great Raider players exceptional about playing smart, but their game preparation was impeccable. In many cases, it was hall of fame preparation, which is exactly what our next chapter is all about.

10
Game Preparation

Preparing for game day mentally is just like preparing for it physically; you must have a plan. Whenever you want to accomplish anything, you should start with the end product in mind. This is a thought process I was taught in my Oakland Raider years with Bill Callahan and Al Davis, and it really makes sense. What do you want to accomplish? What is your ultimate goal? Start with your final goal in mind and work backward. Make sure you create a detailed checklist of the steps you have to take along the way to accomplish your goal.

Football is like baseball; you have to know what to do in every specific situation. At the college and professional levels, the players' goal every week is to be as prepared as possible for every situation.

Practice is a major component of a player's game preparation—and probably the most important. Players react best to the things they have done over and over again in practice. Coaches can talk about a lot of things and alert players to be ready for this and that, but the bottom line is that players remember most what they execute in practice.

"Know your enemy and know yourself and you can fight a hundred battles without disaster."

Sun Tzu

Anticipation and Recognition

Film study is another component to a player's weekly game preparation. This all started with hall of fame coach Paul Brown. He was one of the first coaches to film practice and study film as a coach and with the team. Many of the modern practices for how football coaches organize and structure their teams came from the innovative ideas of Coach Brown.

The study of practice and game film has many advantages for players and coaches. First, watching practice film allows you to detail your own team's blocking schemes in the run game. Plus, it allows you to clean up the timing, spacing, and reads in your passing game. Every player can watch himself and see whether he is doing things correctly by performing the right assignment and the right technique. Film study is a tool that enables coaches and players to self-analyze the assignments and techniques they go through in their weekly preparation.

In addition to watching your own team on film, you also need to know your opponent. Knowing your opponent's strengths and weaknesses will allow you to have a clear understanding of what to anticipate from them on game day. Studying your opponent in detailed situations will help you anticipate and recognize the opponent's reactions in those specific situations.

Those who invest time in their weekly game preparation are a step ahead on game day. Not only do they know what to do and when to do it, but they can also anticipate and react quicker to the opponent's tendencies that they have seen on film. Players who invest in their weekly film preparation are more prepared than those who don't. They know what to expect in each situation. In this chapter, we explore how to watch film as well as how to set up weekly film studies of specific situations.

Paul Brown's Contributions to Football

Paul Brown was a successful high school and college coach before he moved to the professional level and changed the game. He first organized the Cleveland Browns in 1946. Much of the scientific exactness of modern coaching can be attributed to Coach Brown. In taking over the Browns in the new All-American Football Conference in 1946, he started doing things that no pro coach had tried. He was the first coach in professional football to hire a full-time staff. He instituted a system for scouting college players that was never before imagined by other pro teams. He used intelligence testing to gauge a college player's learning potential, used notebooks and classroom techniques exclusively, and was the first to set up complete film clip and statistical studies and to grade his own players based on film study. He was the first coach to take his team to a hotel for home games as well as road games. Much of the modern structure of scientific coaching stems from the practices of Paul Brown. He built a dynasty in Cleveland, posting a 167-53-8 record and four AAFC titles, three NFL crowns, and only one losing season in 17 years.

Weekly Film Preparation

Invest in your weekly film preparation. The college regular season is now 12 games. Some leagues have a conference championship game on top of that, and then if your team has a successful season, you will play in a bowl game sometime after that. The NFL has a 16-game regular season with play-off games to follow. Teams will have to win two or three games to advance through the playoffs and reach the Super Bowl. Over the course of the season, your team will face many different defensive styles. Every week, you must get dialed in to the personnel of the team you are playing against plus get a feel for their fronts, coverages, and pressures.

Every defense has its own personality. They have certain players who make them go. Each team may have its own unique blitz or coverage scheme that they specialize in. Your film study is where you familiarize yourself with these nuances. There are certain things we want to know about a defense every week. It's really a set of questions that players and coaches want to answer to familiarize themselves with the opponent. We put these questions in a weekly film study packet for the players so they can watch film on their own.

Start Early

Film prep starts on a player's day off. During game week, film prep starts on the first day after the last game. Typically, that is a day off for the players. This is usually a day when the players will rest up from the previous game. They may have to see the trainers about any bumps and bruises from the game. In college ball, this is on Sunday after a Saturday game. At the college level, coaches have to give the players one entire day off during the week. Typically, we have taken Sunday off to give the players a chance to sleep in and recover after a hard-fought game. Plus, on game weekends, many of their families have traveled a long way to see them play, so having the day off on Sunday gives the players time to spend with their families before they head back home.

Sunday is an off day from meetings, but it is the perfect day to come in and start your film study for the week. Sunday is a good time to watch film of your next opponent's last three games. Another good option is to watch them play against an opponent that is similar to your team. This is an introductory day for the players to just get familiar with the team that they will play this coming week. It is always great when a player does this on his own or with his teammates. Then, when the player comes in on Monday and the coaches introduce the game plan, the player already has a feel for the personnel and personality of the next opponent.

Film Study Packet

One thing I do that is helpful for players is put together a film study packet. This is basically a template for players on how to watch film during the week. It is something that will build during the week all the way to the game. This packet should mirror the team's weekly preparation so the player has a routine that mirrors the emphasis of the practice that day. That way, he can anticipate the defensive looks he will see in practice. This will further help his recognition and anticipation and make him even more comfortable with what he will see from the opponent. This packet will be the same every week because the information we want to learn about each opponent will be the same. As coaches, we really don't care who we play. They are a nameless, faceless opponent that we want to be totally prepared for every week. We want to know them inside and out, but the most important thing is to make sure that we play at our peak and play mistake free.

The film study packet includes the following sections:

Chart of the Opponent's Last Game

Watching several games of the next opponent is important, but we also want players to chart at least one full game. Charting a game means writing down the critical information on each play. Remember, a college football game averages 72 plays. At the beginning of the season, we create a form that can be used for charting games. This form looks like an Excel worksheet with boxes so you can chart straight down the sheet. For each play, the player charts down and distance, yard line, front, blitz, and coverage. At the college level, we have the games already broken down so that when players watch the film, the defensive front, blitz, and coverage already show up on the film.

Weekly Breakdown

A week before a game, we have our young coaches do a statistical breakdown on at least the last three games of our upcoming opponent. The last game they break down is the last game the opponent played. From this statistical break-down, they enter critical information into a computer, which will take the film and cut it up into specific training tapes that the coaches use to form a game plan. From this breakdown, we create situational and formation tapes that the players will study to familiarize themselves with the opponent. At the end of the breakdown, if we need more information on the opponent, we simply add another game to the breakdown until we have the information we need.

"The only place where success comes before work is in the dictionary."

Vidal Sassoon

Formation Study

After the players study a few games, they will study the opponents by formation. They take a detailed look at how the defense lines up against certain formations and personnel groupings. Typically, that's how we start our weekly preparation for Monday practices. We want the players to study the formation on Sunday and Monday nights because that's when we work on it for practice.

Third Down

The next situational area we address after the normal down and formational plays is the third-down package. Typically, this includes third and long (10 yards or more), third and 7 to 10 yards, third and medium (4 to 6 yards), third and 2 or 3 yards, and third and 1 yard. We have film cutups that reflect these situations and build tendencies for the defense indicating what we will see on those down and distances. We begin working on third-down situations on a Tuesday practice in a college work week. The players should study the third-down cutups on Monday night or Tuesday before a Tuesday work practice.

Red Zone

The red zone is the area we designate as the 20-yard line to about the 12-yard line on the opponent's end of the field. In this area, we use some field plays, but we also use some specific plays designed to beat the defenses we see in this area of the field. The film study should tell us what the personality of the defense is in this area of the field.

Tight Zone

This is the area from the 12-yard line to the goal line. Many defenses change personalities inside this area of the field. Some have certain coverages that they rely on. Others blitz more and take more chances in this area because they are working on a shorter field and they have less area to cover. In any event, we need to be exact on the defensive looks we will see. This is the scoring zone, and these plays will be critical to the outcome of the game. Typically, we will work on these tight-zone plays in our Wednesday practice. Therefore, players should watch these tight-zone plays on film by Wednesday.

Short Yardage and Goal Line

A short-yardage play is considered third and 1, and goal line is considered from the 3-yard line to the goal line. These are two specific situations that should be watched separately. Depending on the week, there may be some carryover on how the offense attacks these defenses. Depending on the offensive personnel on the field, there may be some carryover on the defenses in these areas.

Two-Point Defenses

Players always need to know what to expect from the opponent in two-point situations. Typically, this will fall in the tight-zone area of the situational game.

Questions to Ask During Film Study

Many of the questions you need to ask about the opponent will be the same from week to week. Here are some of the questions that a receiver needs to ask in his film study through the week:

- What are their top three coverages overall?
- Do they like to blitz? What part of the field and when?
- Do their corners play right and left or do they flip?
- Do their corners play field and boundary?
- Do their linebackers play to strong and weak or field and boundary?
- How do their corners play? Are they soft or aggressive?
- Do they play much man coverage?
- Are they physical when they play man?
- Who is their best cover guy in the secondary?
- Who is the weak link in the secondary?
- Who is the best tackler in the back end?
- Is there a secondary player they like on the blitz?
- Who is their nickel player?
- Do they corner blitz?
- Do they play corners over versus slot formations?
- Do they like to zero blitz (blitz with no safety in the hole)? If so, where will they do that?
- How do they handle blocking on the perimeter?
- How does their secondary handle play-action passes?
- How do their secondary players handle double moves?
- Do they use their hands to play off blocks?
- Do they do a good job of communicating on defense?
- Are they very experienced in the back end?
- Do they have any rookies or young players starting or playing in the secondary?

These are just a few of the questions that a player would like to know about the opponent. A key to offensive football is the ability to have some certainty about how the defense will react when the offense puts them in a certain situation. Knowing the answers ahead of time will give the player a lot of confidence going into the contest that he really knows his opponent.

Testing Players

Over my coaching career, I have helped players prepare for upcoming games by giving them a written test at the end of each week. This tests their critical knowledge of the opponent as well as their understanding of the game plan. This test has evolved over the years. Typically, it is a review of the key points of the week. I want players to know the names and numbers of who they are playing. I want them to understand the top fronts and coverages that we will play against. The players need to understand and review the important coaching points for our top plays, especially in our situational packages. If there is a special play in the tight zone or on third down, the test reflects that and makes the players realize the importance of that play in that situation. I work any special tips and reminders in to the test so the test becomes a great review at the end of the week in preparation for the game.

I take notes on every practice. I have those notes typed, and I give the players a copy at the end of the week as they prepare for the game. The notes include information on all the corrections made in practice during the week, and this provides a great review for game day. These notes enable players to learn from their own mistakes as well as from the mistakes of other players.

I learned a valuable lesson as a coach when I was with the Indianapolis Colts in the late 1990s under Jim Mora. I worked with a very experienced staff there. Tom Moore, an ex-Iowa Hawkeye and veteran NFL coordinator, was the offensive coordinator. Gene Huey was the running backs coach. He had spent years with Nebraska and also developed NFL players Marshall Faulk and Edgerrin James, just to name a couple. Bruce Arians was the quarterbacks coach. He did a great job with Peyton Manning as a rookie and in his early years before moving on to become a coordinator with the Pittsburgh Steelers and win a Super Bowl. The tight ends coach was Tony Marciano, and the line coach was Howard Mudd. Coach Mudd is one of the great offensive line coaches in the NFL. He played in the NFL for many years and has coached for many more. I learned a lot about football from Coach Mudd. I also learned a lot about dealing with players from Coach Mudd. Coach Mudd was really in tune with how his players learned and took in information. He believed that different people learned differently. Coaches have to understand the different ways people learn. One day I was grading my test, and I gave him a copy because I wanted to get his opinion on what I was testing the players on. He looked at it for a while and said to me, "Remember, the test is for the teacher." I'll never forget that statement. He was reminding me that the test is the gauge to find out what I have actually taught the player throughout the week. The test is really more about the teacher than it is about the student. I have always carried that thought with me.

Players Need Space

Players should be given some space before the game. Coach Mudd believed that players needed to be totally prepared, but at a certain point, they needed to be alone in their own thoughts to prepare to play the game. Early in my coaching career, I used to give players a test the night before the game. They would take it to their rooms and complete it that night. I would get it from them at breakfast the next morning and would correct it while they were eating. I stopped doing that once I visited with Howard. Now I give players their test two days before the game. I correct the test the day before the game so the players have time to review any corrections. The night before the game, the player can relax, review any notes and game plans, and get mentally prepared for the game. We finalize some of the preparation earlier, and the players get to be alone in their thoughts and get themselves ready for kickoff. This provides a more relaxed atmosphere for the players getting ready to play.

Summary

When you have coached the game for 25 years and played it for another 10 to 15 years before that, game preparation becomes a very special ritual. In many ways, it's a way of life. It becomes a rhythm of life. Preparation wins games. Every week, players must invest in film preparation if they want to play well. Some of my greatest memories are putting in the extra time before a big game. After a tough week of preparation, it is a great feeling the day before the game when you are prepared for a great game. There is such a feeling of satisfaction to having that work done and knowing you have done all you can to get ready for the opponent. In our next chapter, we will dive into the playbook and explore some of the most popular pass patterns and schemes that are used to attack the field in today's game.

11
Pass Schemes

The passing game is about applying certain concepts to certain defensive coverages. The passing game is about receiver spacing on the field with specific depth and timing. The quarterback's drops must marry with the depth of the receivers' routes. That timing and spacing are critical to the success of the passing game. Bill Walsh once said that the success of the passing game is directly related to the discipline of the receivers and quarterback. The wide receivers make all those lines in the playbook come alive! This chapter is dedicated to the basic pass principles in the passing game that offenses use to attack defenses.

Route Depth

The depths of the routes must marry with the quarterback's drop so the timing of the passing game matches up. On all routes, the receiver needs to come open when the quarterback is ready to deliver the football.

Drops are modified when the quarterback is in the shotgun. For example, a hitch route (figure 11.1) is 6 yards from the line of scrimmage. Under center, the quarterback's drop is three steps, plant, and throw. The drop is modified when the quarterback is in the shotgun. In the shotgun, the three-step drop is changed to one step, plant, and throw. This is a consistent formula in transferring the drop of the quarterback in the passing game. Players and coaches must understand this aspect of the passing game.

An effective passing attack is one that attacks the whole field both vertically and horizontally. You want to make the defense respect you and make them protect and defend the whole field. That's why an effective passing game must have several ways to attack the defense.

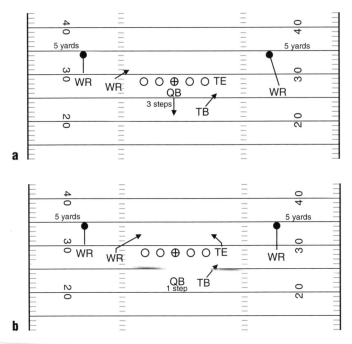

FIGURE 11.1 Hitch route: *(a)* quarterback under center; *(b)* shotgun formation.

Favorite Pass Schemes

- Quick game, including hitches and slants
- Intermediate out cuts
- Curls
- Shallow crossing game
- Deep crossing game
- Vertical passing game
- Movements
- Play-action pass
- Screens

Sequence of Every Pattern

Each pattern is its own specific play that should be learned individually. Every pattern has its own rules specific to that pattern, so players should learn the patterns separately and specifically. Coaches should try to follow a sequence, and every pass play should have a primary, alternate, and outlet receiver for the quarterback. The *primary receiver* is the one whom the play is designed for. The *alternate receiver* is there as the quarterback's second option if the primary receiver is not open. The *outlet receiver,* often called the flare control, is always a third option. The outlet receiver is often a back out of the backfield or a tight end to whom the quarterback can drop the ball if the first two options aren't available.

The great quarterbacks know their options and often make huge plays by giving the ball to the outlets when the opportunity presents itself. All players must understand the timing and know when they are designed to come open. Quarterbacks must study every play so they understand where to send the ball—first to the primary receiver, then the alternate, and finally the outlet.

Quick Game

The quick game (figure 11.2) is a good way to throw the ball out to the perimeter quickly and put it into the receiver's hands. The ball must be delivered on time and accurately. The receiver needs to run a disciplined route, and the quarterback must use quick footwork and deliver an accurate, firm ball.

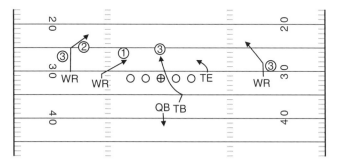

FIGURE 11.2   Quick-game slants.

Hitches

Hitches are great versus coverage that is soft outside such as Cover 3 when the defense is loaded up on the run. Hitches are also good versus a blitz when the coverage is soft outside. Hitch routes are relatively easy balls to throw and catch. This pass should be thrown for a high percentage. It is fairly easy to throw versus off coverage. This is a route that is often used as an audible versus a blitz.

Hitches typically convert to fades versus cloud coverage or Cover 2. The hitch game is a great option versus off coverage, but it doesn't adjust well to a variety of coverages.

Slants

Slants are great routes because the pattern can adjust to almost any coverage. Another good thing about the slant route is that this route can be effective in almost every situation. It's a good route on first and 10, and many coaches like it on a variety of third downs. Some coaches like running slants even on third and long because they believe that these are high-percentage throws. Another key element is that the receiver will be catching the ball while moving forward.

The slant route can be taught in many ways. The coach must decide how to run the slant route so the quarterbacks and receivers are on the same page. The team's personnel may be a factor in whether the team runs a lot of slant routes. Typically, big and strong receivers are better slant runners than smaller, slightly built receivers. Teams that have a big, strong receiver may like the matchup.

Receivers must learn to break off the slant route in front of the defensive back. When running the slant route versus off coverage, the receiver must flatten out the route and beat the defender to the ball on his angle to the quarterback. Versus press technique, some teams like to let the receiver widen, sell the fade, and then slip back underneath the defensive back when he turns his hips to run with the fade. Others teach the receiver to bust off versus press coverage, beating the defensive back off the line of scrimmage to the inside and creating separation.

When the receiver is working off the line of scrimmage versus press coverage, the key for the quarterback is to understand the receiver's problems, sink on the third step, and allow the receiver to win the race before delivering the football. The timing is different for the quarterback than it is when the receiver has off coverage and the quarterback throws on a three-step, plant, and throw motion.

Intermediate Out Cuts

Intermediate 12-yard out cuts are timing routes that attack the outside flats of the defensive coverage. Like hitch routes, outs are used to attack the soft zone outside versus Cover 3 or off coverage (figure 11.3). Like hitches, out routes are also good versus the blitz when off coverage is used. Out cuts are typically converted to fades versus cloud coverage or Cover 2.

Out cuts fall into a category of routes called individual cuts. Individual cuts are single routes that are good versus single coverage. Outs, hooks, curls, and comebacks are considered individual cuts.

The timing on the out cut is critical. The ball must be thrown before the receiver makes his break. From under center, the quarterback's drop should be five steps, plant, and throw. The quickness and the timing of the drop are more important than depth. The quarterback should take the quickest five steps he can and get the ball out! From the shotgun, the quarterback's drop would be three steps, plant, and throw.

Not all teams have out cuts as a part of their passing attack. A lot of very successful passing teams don't throw out cuts. For the out cut, we teach the receiver to use a seven-step rollover speed cut to the sideline; the seventh step is an angle step to the boundary. The top of the route should look like an upside down J. The receiver should get friendly back to the quarterback at the end of the out cut.

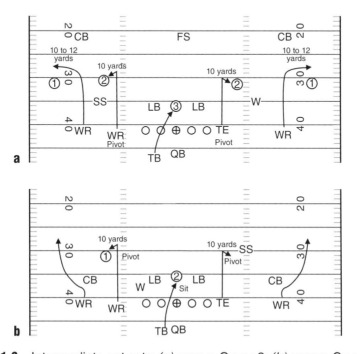

FIGURE 11.3 Intermediate out cuts: *(a)* versus Cover 3; *(b)* versus Cover 2.

Our receivers run their out cuts at the outside hip of the outside zone defender in order to maintain leverage on the out breaking route. That way, the receiver can run away downhill to the boundary, away from the outside zone defender who is playing corner.

Some coaches teach conversions on out cuts versus press; others teach their receivers to keep the out cut on versus man as long as it's not rotation. When receivers get good at running outs versus a Cover 1 corner, this can be a great route; however, a lot of technique work in one-on-one situations is required to help the quarterback gain confidence in throwing this pass.

Curls

The concept of the curl route is as old as the passing game itself, but it is still very effective. Curls are a basic pattern used in almost every passing offense.

For the quarterback, this is a five-step hitch throw. It is a real rhythm throw for the quarterback when under center. In the shotgun, it would be a three-step hitch throw. Our curls are 12-yard routes that come back downhill to 10 yards, right back at the quarterback (figure 11.4). The receivers must get good at bursting and then turning with their shoulder pads over their toes. The receiver should put his outside foot, or break foot, at 12 yards and come straight back to the quarterback.

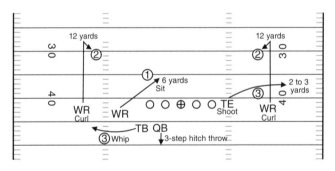

FIGURE 11.4 Curl route.

Shallow Crossing Game

The shallow crossing game is a great complement to the vertical game because it attacks the field horizontally. The shallow crossing game gives the quarterback a running receiver who is crossing the underneath zone (figure 11.5). Typically, versus zone, these routes give the quarterback a triangle read that puts pressure on the defense to play discipline in their zone coverages.

Many coaches like the shallow crossing routes versus man coverage because these routes give the receiver a chance to run away from the man across the field. These routes can also be an equalizer for a team that doesn't have a lot of speed at receiver, providing ways for those players to get open versus man coverage. These are big catch and run plays in which the receiver is counted on to gain yards after making the catch on the run.

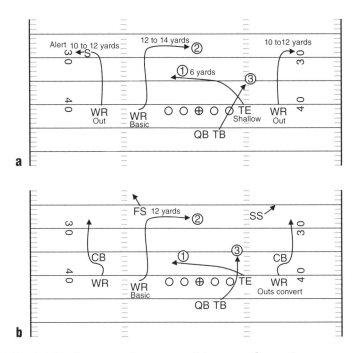

FIGURE 11.5   *(a)* Shallow crossing game; *(b)* versus Cover 2.

Deep Crossing Game

The deep crossing routes are those that hit in the 16- to 18-yard area. These routes get a big chunk of yardage and usually attack the defense at three different levels. Typically, one receiver takes the top off the coverage, the next crosses the field in that 16- to 18-yard range, and another receiver is some kind of flare control underneath to control the underneath coverage (figure 11.6).

The great thing about the crossing game is that a receiver may not be open initially, but if he just keeps running, he will run into an open area. If the quarterback can hang on, the receiver will eventually run into an open area of the defense.

In the deep crossing route shown in figure 11.6, the wide receiver on the 16- to 18-yard crossing route is the primary receiver, the tight end on the shallow cross is the alternate receiver, and the fullback on the read route is the outlet receiver. The quarterback starts under center, takes seven steps, and then fakes the lead draw. The post route is what we call an alert. The quarterback can peek at the post when the middle of the field is open.

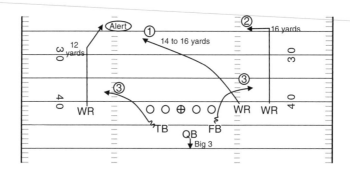

FIGURE 11.6 Deep crossing game.

Vertical Passing Game

The vertical passing game typically includes go balls (figure 11.7) and four verticals (figure 11.8). These vertical passes set up all the other passes in the passing game. When the defense has to respect the vertical passes, this makes it easier for the receivers to get open on the shorter and intermediate routes.

Go balls (figure 11.7) may seem simple, but receivers must master some important techniques for running a go ball. The receiver should run the defender down and try to step on his toes. The receiver shouldn't break

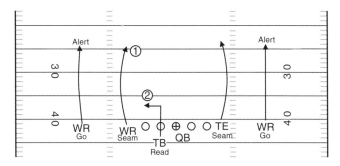

FIGURE 11.7   Go-ball play in the vertical passing game.

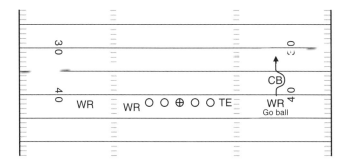

FIGURE 11.8   Four verticals.

until he can smell the defender's breath; in other words, the receiver wants to get right up on top of the defender before making the break to go by him. Then, when going by the defender, the receiver should get on top of the defender as quickly as possible and get the defender on train tracks (i.e., get the defender directly behind him and keep his body in between the ball and the defender). The wide receiver wants to get back on top of the defender as he tries to go by him.

Four verticals (figure 11.8) force the defense to defend all four receivers deep vertically. The threat of all four receivers going deep is something that the offense must make the defense respect. If the offense can do this, it will make everything else they are trying to do in the passing game easier. The outside wide receivers are on alert versus their matchups. The primary receiver is the slot on the seam. The alternate is the read route.

The vertical passing game has to be a threat in order for the rest of your passing game to be effective. If the defense doesn't respect your vertical passing game, the defenders will tend to sit on your intermediate passing game and make it more difficult for your receivers to get open on their individual cuts.

Movements

Movements are throws on which the quarterback's throwing spot is changed up. Changing up the quarterback's throwing spot helps prevent the defense from zeroing in on him on the pass rush. It also forces the defense to keep disciplined pass rush lanes while containing the quarterback. Movements are sprint-outs, so the quarterback and a receiver are on the run and moving away from the defense (figure 11.9). These are great change-of-pace throws that are good versus blitzes and pressure. They are also good change-ups on normal downs as well as in the red zone.

The primary receiver is on the sprint option route. The alternate wide receiver is on the pivot return. The outlet is the quarterback run. On the sprint option, the quarterback wants to open up and sprint out to break contain at a 45-degree angle. The quarterback looks to hit the option on the third step. If the option is not open on the third step, the quarterback stays on the run to find the pivot return.

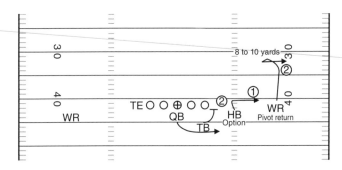

FIGURE 11.9   Sprint option.

Play-Action Pass

Play-action passes (figure 11.10) are executed off the same action and look like the corresponding run game. The passes directly complement the run game, and the run and the pass directly play off each other. The primary wide receiver is on the crack post, the alternate is on the cross, and the outlet (the tailback) is on the check shoot route.

The key to play-action passing is the offensive line and the play fake. The offensive line must come off the ball with low pads and sell the run. If the line pops up on the snap, this doesn't sell run to the defense, and the defense doesn't get the illusion that the play is a run.

The other important factor in the play-action game is how the quarterback and the backs fake the play. The fakes have to be carried out. The backs must come through the line at full speed and keep their pads low. They should not stop or look back after the exchange. They have to carry out the fake and make the defense think they have the ball.

Depending on the action, the quarterback will use his shoulders to crouch slightly on the exchange. Often, the quarterback can get the safeties to freeze by rolling his shoulders and focusing his eyes on the mesh point with the running back.

The backs and the quarterback must take great pride in their ability to fake in the play-action game. If the runs and the passes look the same, the offense can generate huge passing plays in the play-action game.

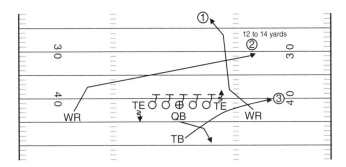

FIGURE 11.10   Play-action pass.

Screens

Teams use various types of screens, including tailback screens and wide receiver screens. An offense may run bubble screens, tunnel screens, quick screens to the backs, or two-count screens to the backs.

Screens are great rush control plays because they play off the aggressiveness of the defensive rush. If your team becomes good at running screens, you give the pass rushers something else to think about besides hitting the quarterback. They have to be concerned with redirecting to the quickly thrown ball. Wide receiver screens (figure 11.11) are good because they don't require a lot of blocking; plus, these screens get the ball into an athletic player's hands in space. The offense doesn't have to execute many critical blocks before they can make yardage. Wide receiver screens put a lot of pressure on the perimeter defense to rally and make tackles. The more spread oriented a team is, the more wide receiver screens become part of their package. Spread teams often view these screens as runs. Screens are high-percentage throws for a quarterback who is used to getting the ball out of his hands quickly and controlling the rush.

On the wide receiver quick screen, the wide receiver jabs and comes back inside the wing's block. The play-side guard slips and releases to the play-side linebacker. The center slips and releases to the near cornerback.

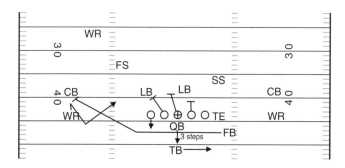

FIGURE 11.11 Wide receiver quick screen.

Spacing

Overall, the passing game is built on timing, accuracy, and spacing. Different route combinations rely on splits, depths, and spacing. Receivers must have consistency and discipline in route running and spacing for the passing game to be efficient. The receivers must understand the spacing on each particular route, and they must be on the same page with the quarterback on all coverage adjustments.

Good quarterbacks are accurate throwers. The more experience quarterbacks get, the more they learn to throw away from defenders in zone coverage. The great passing teams have a quarterback who throws away from defenders, and they have receivers who come back to the football. Regardless of how good the coverage seems to be, great passing teams complete a lot of passes because their players know how to throw and catch.

The coach should tell receivers what he wants and make them do it right. Sometimes receivers are guilty of cutting their routes short. This is a common problem that happens everywhere. I have heard some coaches say that if you want a 16-yard route, you should tell the receivers 18 and you'll get 16. This type of thinking makes no sense to me. If you made all your football rules like this, you would be modifying everything that you do. I guess I am from the old school. I am from the school of being exact on the football field, of everybody knowing what the depth and rule are for each route. I am from the school of when a coach demands something from a player, he accepts nothing less than what he emphasizes. If a curl route is 12 yards, the player better put his upfield foot at 12 yards and burst and turn back to the quarterback. If the comeback is 16, the player better get 16 and work back down to the boundary. Once a coach says one thing and means something else, where does it end? I like to keep things simple. Mean what you say and say what you mean.

"Tell them exactly what you want and make sure they give it to you."

Veteran NFL line coach Howard Mudd

Number of Passing Schemes

How many concepts do you need? I think the question should be, How many concepts can your quarterback handle and throw well? In football, you should never run more offenses than your quarterback can handle. The coach has to be realistic about the talents, mental capacity, and experience of the quarterback. The coach must also consider the quarterback's arm talent and design the offense on what he does best. That can very well change from year to year based on the quarterback's talent and experience. Coaches can often run many of the same concepts by window-dressing them with different shifts, formations, and personnel groupings. This way the quarterback and receivers can run many of the same concepts while the defense sees a different look.

Passing schemes are successful by application. In the passing game, the offense needs to have concepts that are effective versus the coverages they are seeing. Certain route concepts apply well to certain coverages. The key is to apply the proper passes to the coverages that the defense is using in that particular situation. This can be an oversimplification, but certain routes are built to attack Cover 2, and some routes are man beaters. Applying those routes to those specific coverages is one of the keys to offensive football. Crossing routes are great versus man coverage. The key is having the ability to match your passing patterns to the various coverages you see and having the system flexibility to run the right play at the right time to take advantage of what the defense is giving you. Players must have the ability to make the proper adjustments to execute versus the coverage that they see.

Summary

Over the years, I have been lucky to observe and be part of some of football's great passing teams. As a member of the coaching staffs for the Indianapolis Colts and Oakland Raiders, I competed against Dan Marino and Tom Brady, who were and are amazing players. I spent four years with Peyton Manning and Marvin Harrison in Indianapolis. I spent two years with Rich Gannon and Jerry Rice with the Raiders. Gannon was the MVP in 2002 when I was with the Raiders. All these players had an amazing understanding of the passing game. Their sense of timing and anticipation were at a whole other level. They knew how to exploit the defensive coverage with the appropriate route combination.

We have talked about understanding coverages. These great players knew their patterns inside and out, and they knew how to exploit the defense with a specific route combination. They were also experts on their own strengths and weaknesses as well as the weaknesses of the defense. Seeing the pages of a playbook brought to life by truly talented and gifted players is a thing of beauty.

In the next chapter, we will explore the championship mind-set. Everything that players and coaches do is to prepare to win championships. We will explore the pursuit of the ultimate prize and the mind-set required to make it to the top of the heap.

12

Championship Mind-Set

This chapter is about having the championship mentality. The best players apply a certain attitude and pride to their work. They know that there is no substitute for attention to details and simple hard work. The very best know that the mastery of the smallest details will not fail them in that moment of truth when the game is in the balance. Playing your best when your best is needed—that's what is expected in playing for championships!

Focus on the Process

At the college or professional level, a football season is truly a process. It is a calendar year during which you do certain things just to give yourself an opportunity to play for your ultimate goal in the fall. The process is the yearly schedule under which the coaching staff works. In this chapter, we focus on the process from training camp to the end of the season.

One of the worst things a team can do is get ahead of itself. In this age of media, everybody wants to talk about who is the best and who is ranked where. In the grand scheme of things, it really doesn't matter. Most people not involved will want to put the cart before the horse because that's what media types do. Coaches and players are held accountable for how we perform on game day, and at the end of the season, we tally up all those game days to create a report card, and that record is what you are—good, bad, or average.

The key is to stay focused on the process along the way. History tells us that the most prepared teams and the most tough-minded teams increase their odds of winning. Coaches are constantly trying to encourage players and teams to do all they can in their preparation. You have to walk before you can run.

I like to establish a weekly routine. We start this routine in training camp and commit to it for the entire year. That routine includes the film we watch every week, the drills we commit to doing before and after practice, and the things that will separate our team and players from the rest of the teams we will play this fall. After establishing this routine, we trust it and focus on the details of that routine throughout the year. There's an old cowboy saying, "You can't ride 'em in the chutes!" This refers to the cowboys in the rodeo. It means you can't ride a bucking bronco until they open the door. When you're in the chutes, you should relax until the action starts. It's the same with football. In college, games are usually on Saturday, so you shouldn't worry about playing the game until kickoff on Saturday. On Monday, make sure all your focus is on your Monday routine. The same can be said for Tuesday, Wednesday, and Thursday because the things you need to get done on those days will properly prepare you for the main event on Saturday. Focus on the process and stay in the moment. When you do that, good things will happen for your team in the long run.

Accept Constructive Criticism

Bill Belichick is one of the great coaches of our time. When he talks about the personality of a championship team, one thing he mentions is that to be a good player or team, you have to be able to accept constructive criticism. "I don't know how you can improve unless you can accept constructive criticism," he once said.

> **"What a football team has to do is accept constructive criticism, recognize what it didn't do well or what its weaknesses are, and then improve on them to get better."**
>
> *New England Patriots head coach Bill Belichick*

No player or team is perfect. The teams that ultimately have the most success are ones that improve their weaknesses and make critical changes along the way. Every week, coaches review the game tape and show the players what they did well along with the areas that they can improve for the next week. Players must learn to accept constructive criticism and make the adjustments that the coaches would like the players to make. Players need to look realistically at their performance and make the necessary adjustments, understanding that this will improve their performance from week to week. Players who don't accept criticism will not improve at the same rate, and their performance will eventually cost the team at some point during the season.

Work Hard to Improve Faster

The harder you work, the faster you improve. In 1998, I was hired by the Indianapolis Colts to coach their wide receivers. It was Jim Mora's first year as head coach, and going into the draft, Indianapolis had the very first pick. As an organization, we needed a quarterback, and we were looking at the two top quarterbacks in the draft. The first was Peyton Manning, the senior from Tennessee who was the son of the great Archie Manning. The other was Ryan Leaf. Leaf had led Washington State to the Rose Bowl as a junior. The evaluation was a fascinating one, and I learned a lot about player intangibles. In the end, that was the difference between the two quarterbacks. Manning is one of the greatest players to ever play the game. Leaf has been out of the league for some time.

Peyton Manning's work ethic has become part of his legacy, and it was really something to see when he was a young professional. Drafted number 1 overall, Peyton started as a rookie. I'll never forget his first eight games as a rookie. He was horrible, to say the least. He would show real signs of promise at times, but overall he made way too many mistakes to give the team a chance to win. Interceptions and mental errors at the worst possible times were a trademark of his game for the first eight games of his rookie year.

All through the first part of the season, Peyton was disappointed in his play, but he never got discouraged. Through all the disappointment, the losses, and the criticism—and believe me, there were a lot of critics—he never stopped believing that things would get better. More important, he focused on the work. He worked on improving his reads on the field. He worked on reading coverages in the film room. He stayed after practice and threw balls to the receivers. He worked day and night on and off the field. He worked harder than anyone else on the team. And guess what started to happen in the second half of the season. It was one of the most amazing transformations I have ever witnessed in coaching. Peyton started making plays. Not all at once, but gradually he started playing more consistently. By December, he looked like a different player. He was visibly bigger and stronger. His deep ball was tight and more accurate, and his confidence was like night and day. This young player was so driven. It's the greatest example I have ever seen of simple hard work. It became clear to me that, in the words of Tom Moore, our veteran offensive coordinator, "The player who works the hardest improves the fastest!" Moore made that statement at the end of Peyton's rookie year. This was obvious to everyone who witnessed his transformation that year.

This statement is so true. The harder you work, the faster you get better. That's why the quality of work ethic is so important in young players and teams. That's why hard work and toughness often beat talent, especially when talent doesn't work hard.

Think Team First

In September 2001, I was coaching with the Indianapolis Colts. It was week 3 of the season, and we were on the road playing an 0-2 New England Patriots team. This was Bill Belichick's second season in New England, and the Pats seemed to be in a tough stretch. In training camp, they lost a coach when 45-year-old Dick Rehbein died of cardiac arrest on August 6. In week 2, the Patriots' franchise quarterback Drew Bledsoe was severely injured when he sheared a blood vessel in his chest after being tackled out of bounds by Mo Lewis of the Jets.

I was in the press box during the game against the Patriots. I'll never forget the pregame. In those days, the NFL would usually pick one side of the ball to introduce before the game. Because we were the road team, we went first. They introduced the entire Colts offense, and of course, the last player to be introduced was Peyton Manning. What happened next was subtle at the time, but it may have been a signal of something really special. The announcer started calling out the Patriots' starters on defense. He called Bryan Cox and Willie McGinnis, but nothing happened. He called Mike Vrabel, Ty Law, but still nothing happened. Once the announcer finished calling the whole defensive unit, the entire unit ran out together. It didn't seem significant at the time, but looking back at it in hindsight, it was very significant.

On that same day, a sixth-round draft pick from Michigan made his first start for the injured Bledsoe. Tom Brady beat us that day, and he went on to win three of his first four starts. Brady set a record for not throwing an interception in his first 162 attempts as a starter, which was pretty impressive. Later that season, when Bledsoe was healthy enough to play again, Belichick decided to stay with Brady as the starter—and the rest is history. The Patriots went on to upset the St. Louis Rams in the Super Bowl that year. People called the Rams the greatest show on turf, and the Rams were heavy favorites in the big game that year, but they got beat by a better team. As I watched the Super Bowl and they announced the teams, I just shook my head when they introduced the Patriots defense and the players all ran on to the field together as one unit. I wasn't surprised by the result when Vinatieri kicked the game winner to give New England their first Super Bowl championship.

Never Stay Down

In the old west, they called it grit. A movie was made about it. Coach Parcells talked to our Oklahoma team before the national championship game with Florida, and the last thing he said was this: To win the big game, you got to have a big pair. Players must find a competitive toughness in order to win when things get tough.

> **"Only a man who knows what it is like to be defeated can reach down to the bottom of his soul and come up with the extra ounce of power it takes to win when the match is even."**
>
> *Muhammad Ali*

There is an old saying in football, "It's not for everybody." To play this game, you have to love it. If you don't love the game, it's really difficult to play. Football is the only game where somebody gets knocked down on almost every play. That doesn't happen in any other sport. As mentioned earlier, the first drill that most players are taught in the game of football is up-downs or Lombardis. Football is a tough game, and you're going to get knocked down, so you better learn to get back up again.

When I was a kid, my father told me, "If you get in a fight and you get knocked down, don't ever stay down. You could get kicked, or stomped, you could really be hurt. Always get up as soon as you can." It's the same in football. The only guys who never get knocked down in football are the ones who don't play. You have to learn to get up when you get knocked down—as a player and as a team. Just like in life, you are going to get beat now and then, but you have to get back up and dust yourself off and get back in the fight. That's what good teams do when they lose or have a bad day. They shake themselves off and get back at it. That's how coaches and veteran players often show good leadership. It's easy to find leaders when things are going well, but true leadership emerges when your team hits a bump in the road; these players fight to stay the course, believe in the plan, and more important, believe in each other. One of the most satisfying parts of coaching is when a team loses a tough game and everyone gets down on them, but the team sticks together, rights the ship, and finishes as a champion—proving everyone wrong. That is the best feeling in sports because the only people who believed in the team were the players and coaches in that locker room. Always get right back up when you get knocked down, and then dig down and come back even stronger.

Champions know the difference between pain and injury. In over a quarter of a century of coaching and playing ball at every level, I have observed that one thing is true of every champion. Champions play with pain.

Pain is something that is uncomfortable for you. Pain is an irritant. Champions realize that a football season is long and that the games are physical. The tough competitive games take a physical toll on the body. Every player who played significant snaps is sore for a couple days after the game. As the season goes along, sometimes players don't heal up totally before the next week's game. Good players find a way to play and perform even when they aren't 100 percent.

Injury is a different thing. Injury is a physical condition that will not allow you to perform at a competitive level. No player should play if he is injured. Football is a tough enough game to play even when you are 100 percent. A player who isn't healthy enough to protect himself on the field should not play. If you play football, you will get bumps and bruises at some point; it is just the nature the game. The only players who are immune from injury are the ones who don't play in games.

Focus on the Details

The difference is in the details. People often ask me what made some of the great players I have known so great. I can take three players, for example. I spent four years with Peyton Manning with the Indianapolis Colts. I spent two years with Jerry Rice and Rich Gannon of the Oakland Raiders. In 2002, Rich Gannon was MVP of the NFL. If I had to compare these great players and talk about what made each one great, I would say that each one of them took no shortcuts. They were obsessed with the details of their play. Whether it was studying film or working a technique, each one of them was driven to do it better than anyone else. They were masters at their trade. They didn't care how long it took in the film room or the practice field. They were determined to get it done better than anyone else. They knew that when the bright lights came on, the difference would be in the details.

Players on great teams put pressure on each other. A standard of play is expected from championship teams. Older players will accept nothing else. That work ethic is passed on to the younger players. Practice becomes just like the game. Pete Rose said, "Practice the game the way you're going to play the game. Practice hard and play hard." It's the only way. It has to be that way if you are going to play at your highest level.

Be a Good Teammate

What does it mean to be a good teammate? Being a good teammate means a lot of things. Simply being helpful to another player on the team is being a good teammate. It may be watching film and helping a young player understand a certain route concept. Helping another player learn the signals is another way.

We have freshmen join our college team every year. We don't allow hazing. That means we don't allow the older players to play tricks on the young guys as a fraternity does. We want our older players to help the young guys understand what it takes to be a productive member of the team. The older players should help the young guys learn so they can help us win.

Being a good teammate is going the extra mile to make a new player feel welcome so he can learn the system. It could also mean just picking a guy up when he is feeling down or when he is having a tough day. Everybody has a tough day now and then, but good teams have players who support one another so when those tough days come they can work through it together.

Don't Listen to the Critics

In the 21st century, we live in an electronic age. Everything is news. There are four ESPN channels, along with Facebook, Twitter, and bloggers. And everyone has an opinion about the game of football and who's in it. There are 10 times as many critics as there are players or teams.

We follow one rule: Don't listen to the media, good or bad. They build you up to tear you down. They will go overboard when things are going well, and they will give too much blame when things go badly. The best strategy is to just worry about the players and coaches in that locker room and nobody else. If you keep your focus on your teammates' and coaches' opinions, you will stay level-headed throughout the season.

Players and their families should never read things on the Internet. Even at the high school level today, some players get hundreds of articles written about them on recruiting sites before they ever step foot on a college campus. This is a shame because many of them will get more attention for their potential than they will for what they actually accomplish on the college level.

College coaches constantly talk to players about not reading information on the Internet. We have to talk to players and parents. Sometimes the parents are the worst. They get too caught up in what people are saying about their son, and they let it affect their outlook. I ask players and parents this question: "Why do you care about what some guy sitting in his basement in his underwear thinks about you?" You should only care about what your teammates and coaches think about your performance.

Be Confident, Not Cocky

There is a difference between cocky and confident. Muhammad Ali is one of the great champions of all time and also one of the great competitors. We can learn a lot from Ali. We have heard his famous quotes. He was the poster child for positive self-talk, which is important for all of us for high achievement. Ali would say, "I'm the greatest, the greatest of all time!" But one of his best quotes was this: "I said I was the greatest even before I knew I was!"

"If you even dream of beating me, you'd better wake up and apologize."

Muhammad Ali

Positive thinking and self-affirmation are huge qualities for championship teams. We become what we think of the most. That's why it's so important to fill our minds with positive thoughts. That's what champions do, and in the end, that's where their confidence comes from. No doubt Muhammad Ali was cocky, but more important, he had an inner self-confidence that led him to greatness. That is the ultimate quality that champions and championship teams carry like a chip on their shoulders.

Summary

This chapter contains some of my most cherished feelings about the game. This is a game I have been fortunate to play and coach most of my life. In many ways, it is a way of life for me and my family. The greatness of football is that it is such a brutally difficult game. It is an unforgiving game. As soon as you think you have it made and you relax, somebody will be there to bring you back to earth. One of the things I love about football is the simple, hard unfiltered truth. In the game of football, you don't always get what you want, but most of the time you get what you deserve. It is the only game in which somebody gets knocked down on every play. Therefore, to be the very best, you have to carry the toughest mind-set. It's not the most talented team that wins; it's the most prepared team with the toughest mind-set. It's the team that's obsessed with the details. They just seem to find a way to get the job done. They are a TEAM.

Nothing is more enjoyable for me than to watch a team win a championship. It doesn't matter if it's football, basketball, baseball, or hockey. It doesn't matter if it's high school, college, or the pros. I never get tired of watching the last pitch of any baseball season when a team wins the World Series. Something is so special about the childlike excitement and genuine love the teams share in that moment. Something genuine and pure comes out that touches all of us deep inside. That's why we compete and play the game—the pursuit of those moments. It is a feeling that most people can only dream about.

In our next chapter, we look at the process of the off-season and how players prepare themselves physically for the championship season ahead.

13
Out-of-Season Training

Today, when football season ends, the work starts all over again. This chapter explores the routines that players can use in the out of season. Notice I did not use the term *off-season*. In today's competitive world of sports, there truly is no off-season. If the season isn't going on, you are still working out. This is your out-of-season training. Weight training is important. Strength is one of the most underappreciated attributes that any receiver can possess. Plus, every player should include out-of-season skill development as part of his year-round routine.

> **"People usually know what they should do to get what they want. They just won't pay the price. Understand there is a price to be paid for achieving anything of significance. You must be willing to pay the price."**
>
> *John Wooden in* Wooden: A Lifetime of Observations
> and Reflections On and Off the Court

Out of Season

In college and professional ball, the season ends for most teams in January. In the last couple of years, the NFL has played its Super Bowl in the first week of February, but for most teams the season is over in January. In college ball, a successful season usually ends with a bowl game. After the bowl game, the players get a break for a few weeks and then go back to school in the first couple weeks of January. At this time, the players begin winter conditioning. Winter conditioning is a 6- to 8-week period between the end of the season and spring practice.

Conditioning Seasons During the Out-of-Season Period

Winter conditioning is an all-inclusive training regimen for the entire football team. This is where the work ethic of the team begins to form. At the college level, the rules specify that position coaches cannot work with players during this period of the year except for on-field conditioning. Football-specific work is not allowed by NCAA rule.

At the college level, the next phase of the out-of-season is spring practice. As an assistant coach, I love spring practice because there is no pressure to prepare for a game and all the emphasis is on teaching the players how to play. In spring practice at the college level, we get 15 full practices, and we cover a variety of football situations. Three of the practices have to be nonpadded work by rule. At the end of spring practice, we usually end up with a major scrimmage that is typically called a spring game. Spring practice is valuable because coaches can focus on improving young players and bringing them along in their learning of offensive schemes. The spring game is a great learning situation. Because it is a simulation of a game situation, young players gain experience by playing in front of a crowd. If a player hasn't played much yet in his career, the opportunity to compete in front of a crowd is always good experience. For that reason, the spring game is a valuable part of the out-of-season development.

The next segment of the schedule for the college athlete is summer conditioning. This is basically an 8- to 10-week period when players train together, sacrificing and investing for the season. By the end of summer conditioning, the goal is for the players to be strong, fast, and in great condition for the season ahead. Plus, they want to have the mental toughness as a group to accomplish their goals as a team. A key aspect of summer conditioning is that it is something the team does together. When the players on a team know that they have collectively paid the price in the summer, they will be a difficult team to beat in the fall. A team that works hard together in the summer gains the kind of closeness and cohesiveness that a championship team needs to win the close games in the fall. The summer conditioning routine is one that will prepare players in every way for the rigors of the fall schedule.

Strength Training

Strength training is as important for wide receivers as it is for every player. Strength is an important part of football. When an athlete is stronger, he will see on-the-field benefits in many ways. Receivers have to be strong to get off the line of scrimmage. They have to be strong to block. They have to be strong to battle for the football in one-on-one situations. The other key reason for building strength is to protect the player from injury. Receivers take a lot of collisions. The stronger a player is, the better he can protect himself when running across the middle and taking the physical contact from the defense.

There is also a direct correlation between strength and speed. We are always trying to increase the speed of our athletes. Players who gain strength often gain speed as well. We put our athletes on an all-around weight training program. We want players to be strong in their upper body, shoulders, chest, legs, hips, and hamstrings.

Upper-Body Training

Our players use a routine in which they work the upper body twice a week. This training includes the bench press, the shoulder press, and exercises for the back, biceps, and triceps. The bench press is the major upper-body movement, and players should set goals to improve their strength on the bench each off-season.

Lower-Body Training

The lower body is just as important as the upper body. Lower-body training includes squats, lunges, quad lifts, hamstring lifts, and calf raises. Strength in the hips, buttocks, and thighs is critical for speed development, and those muscles are trained through our lower-body workouts.

Plyometric Training

Plyometric training is essential for speed development. Drills such as box jumps and other explosive actions help players develop the ability to perform explosive movements. Bounds and jumps are great for speed development, and they are a huge part of the year-round training program. Football is filled with explosive movements. Explosive short bursts happen all over the field on game day. These plyometric movements apply directly to what happens on the field.

Resistance Running

The modern athlete has many training devices at his disposal. One of those is resistance bands. Resistance bands are used by track athletes and sprinters to create resistance that causes them to work even harder. This resistance builds strength, which makes the runner stronger and faster when the resistance is detached.

The same can be said for weighted jackets. Our athletes run with weighted jackets to give them added resistance and make their legs stronger and better conditioned. They run sprints, do box jumps, and even run stadium stairs with the weighted vests on to help overall strength and conditioning.

"Fatigue makes cowards of us all."

Vince Lombardi

Hill Running

Running a hill requires both physical and mental endurance. A hill is a challenge, an obstacle that must be conquered. Running up a hill is difficult, which is why it has been such a good training tool over the years. The first time I heard of a player running a hill for conditioning was when I saw a story on the great Walter Payton, the hall of fame running back for the Chicago Bears. Payton's conditioning was famous. As a player for the Bears in the 1970s and mid-1980s, he was considered one of the great conditioned athletes of his time. I remember Walter being interviewed about running this hill back in Mississippi. He would wait until the hottest part of the day, and he would sprint up this mountain. He did it for years, and it became his edge both physically and mentally. Not only did it make him tough physically, but the mental edge it gave him prepared him mentally for a long, tough season.

Our players run hills, and they also run stairs and the parking structure. One of the highlights of the summer for the players is when they sprint up the parking structure from the bottom to the top, which is about four stories in all.

Walter Payton knew that no one worked harder than he did to prepare for the season. He was determined to show the world how great he was. He was driven to be the very best. Years later, Roger Craig and Jerry Rice did the same thing. They were both driven to make sure they were ready for the challenges of the season.

When you invest so much in your off-season training, you are difficult to beat in the fall because you have put so much work in that you just won't give in that easily. That's why in football you have to be in great condition first before anything else. Muhammad Ali said that he would already have the fight won well before he got into the ring. He would win it on the road during early-morning running sessions. When he invested the time, the fight was already won.

"The fight is won or lost far away from witnesses, behind the lines, in the gym, and out there on the road, long before I dance under those lights."

Muhammad Ali

Conditioning and Running

Football is a series of bursts and sprints, so players need to run when preparing for the season. All distances are good for training, whether it's 10-yard sprints or 100-yard sprints. To work on conditioning, players should also get on a track and run longer distances such as 200s and 400s. Receivers must be able to run all day without getting tired. Being challenged at different distances in the summer and out-of-season training will help a player's overall conditioning in the fall.

Position-Specific Drills

We used to call these grass drills or agilities. They are a huge part of the out-of-season training ritual. Drills such as bag drills, high knees, shuffle, and backpedal are general drills that all players need to master. Along with the bag drills common to all positions are the drills covered earlier in the book. These are also good in the out-of-season routine. All of our hand drills can be incorporated into this position-specific section of training. High hands, low hands, quick swim, forearm pull, and shove and quick swim are great drills to incorporate into a position-specific routine a couple times a week in the summer. The next area would be route running drills. The box drill, diagonal cone drill, and all drills that include change of direction and body movement are great to incorporate into a position-specific summer routine a couple times a week.

Routes on Air

Good quarterbacks and receivers play catch year-round. In the summer, the quarterbacks and receivers should run routes on their own and continue to work on the timing and accuracy of the routes they will use in the fall. The only way they can get good at running routes and throwing the ball is by doing it over and over. In the summer, players are on their own, but it is just like playing pickup basketball. They meet at the field and play catch, working on various routes a couple times a week. This is how timing is built in the passing game. When running routes, the receivers should work at game speed so the quarterback and receivers are on the same page and the timing is the same as it will be in the game.

Group Work

In the off-season, players will sometimes get bored running sprints and lifting weights. They will get together and perform some group work against one another. One-on-ones are great because the receivers get competitive man-to-man work against a live defender. If players can work it out to go against each other at least once a week in the summer, that is great. This will get their competitive juices flowing, and the quarterbacks can never get enough work with a receiver running a man cut on a defender. Every receiver is a little different, and the quarterback needs to learn to read the body language of each of his players.

Another competitive group drill that players can work on during the summer is seven-on-seven. Again, just like a pickup summer basketball game, players are used to setting up a seven-on-seven skeleton and working the passing game between the offense and the defense. There is no better way for players to work on their timing than running routes versus a competitive defense. Plus, the players would much rather work against each other than run sprints or stadium stairs. They can move the ball up and down the field and get all sorts of situational play in over the course of the summer. The group work is an important element of the overall summer training routine.

Leadership

Leadership of a football team is developed in out-of-season training. On every team that I have been part of, we have waited to vote for captains until summer training and training camp were over. That way, the players could see who had really put in the work preparing for the season and which players could be counted on when it mattered most. Leading by example is a huge part of out-of-season training. Ideally, the team has veteran players at every position who will do what is required to train and prepare over the summer for the long season ahead. Consistency is the key; we want players who will show up every day and work. We want guys who come in and want to get the job done, do what is required of them, and don't make excuses. Those are the guys the team will be able to count on in the fall when the going gets tough.

Some of the guys who are the hardest workers are the toughest guys when the games start because they just don't have any quit in them. Our best leaders have been guys who didn't talk about doing it, they just got it done, and they wouldn't ask anyone to do anything they wouldn't do themselves.

The best leaders are tough and courageous. Those qualities show up in the out-of-season training program. These are the days of no bright lights or cameras. There are no fans to cheer you on. This is just the plain hard work that must be done to give your team a chance to compete in the fall. As a player, you have to walk the walk before you can talk the talk, and training and leading by example in the summer are a big part of that process. We used to tell the quarterback that he must first believe in himself before anyone else would believe in him. The other thing we would tell the quarterback is that his day-to-day work ethic must convince his teammates that he can be trusted when all else fails. The only way to get that kind of trust is to be consistent every day.

It is the same with receivers and quarterbacks. Quarterbacks trust the receivers who are consistent in running routes and catching the ball. The guys who show up, who are on time, and who run hard and consistently every day are the ones whom the quarterbacks trust. The only way that receivers and quarterbacks gain that trust is by working together daily in the summer when no one else is around.

Conditioning Test

On the first day back in training camp, we have the players perform a 300-yard shuttle. This is our traditional conditioning test to see who is in shape and ready for training camp. The shuttle is five 60-yard timed sprints. The player must average his 40-yard dash time, and he has to do it twice. For example, an offensive lineman needs to do it in an average of 52 seconds. Tight ends and linebackers have to do it in an average of 48 seconds, and the skill guys, the receivers and defensive backs, have to do it in an average of 46 seconds. Players have to run a 300-yard shuttle in their required time and walk back to the line. They get about a minute of rest between the first run and the second run. At the end of the two runs, the coaches average the times, and the average must fall in the prescribed time for each position. Coaches have used many different conditioning tests over the years, but this one has been so good that we have used it for over 30 years. It has held up over time.

Confidence

If a player has worked and invested in a great summer of training, the end result is that the player has the highest level of confidence going into the year. It is great to see a player who is strong and fit, in great condition, and ready for the challenge of the season. You can see it in how these players carry themselves as they come into camp. You can also see the lack of confidence in the guys who aren't ready, the guys who haven't invested the time and effort over the summer. Players gain a real power of positive energy and confidence from putting in the work and having a great summer of conditioning.

Summary

Conditioning truly shows a player's love and dedication to the game. When it's 112 degrees outside in the middle of June and no screaming fans are there to encourage you to run those stadium stairs, you have to dig deep.

There is no glamour in times like this. When it's 5:30 in the morning in the middle of February, there is no glamour in running agilities and lifting weights. They don't put these highlights on ESPN. Or when your workout is done and it's 115 degrees in the middle of July and all you want to do is go sit in the pool, you push yourself back on the field to run routes and get timing with your quarterback. Out-of-season training can be brutal, but it is always necessary to get where you ultimately want to go. There is simply no easy way to get there.

I have truly enjoyed sharing some of my dearest thoughts and memories about this great game that I have been so lucky to be part of. I have had a love affair with football for close to four decades, and I don't see the end in sight anytime soon. One of my earliest memories is the old NFL films and the great John Facenda. There is this slow-motion picture of a ball in the air, and it is rotating ever so slowly. As the ball rotates in the air with the blue sky behind it, I feel as if I have spent a lifetime chasing those special moments of completing that big play. There is nothing more exciting in football than a perfectly thrown deep ball and a graceful explosive athlete outmaneuvering another athlete to make a huge play. Something magical happens when you see the most explosive athletic players on the field do the most amazing things with the football. I love the game of football. A player or coach can give back to the game by respecting the game—playing and coaching it the way it was meant to be done. We have tried to respect that in this book. That's what being a complete receiver is all about. It's not just about catching and running routes and blocking. It's about showing a total respect for the game by being your very best in all areas. Football is a difficult game, and you don't always get what you want. But in the end, we all get what we deserve. I have spent my life searching for game changers. I have spent my life looking for the guy who can turn the tide on one big play. I have found that there are game changers all around on most of the teams that I've been part of. They show up in the most surprising places, mostly through hard work and detailed persistence. Good luck in your pursuit, and I hope in the end you discover a game changer!

DRILL FINDER

Ball Security

Stance

Catching

Releases

Route Running

Blocking

ABOUT THE AUTHOR

Jay Norvell is one of the most influential coaches in college football, having coached NFL and NCAA stars Reggie Wayne, Ryan Broyles, Sage Rosenfels, Roland Williams, Doug Jolley, Juaquin Iglesias, and Manuel Johnson. The current co-offensive coordinator and coach of wide receivers at the University of Oklahoma, he has helped lead the team to bowl appearances in each of his four years on the OU staff. Before coming to OU, he coached at UCLA, Nebraska, Iowa State, Wisconsin, Northern Iowa, and Iowa. He has coached in nine college bowl games and three BCS games, including the national championship in 2008 with the Oklahoma Sooners, and has coached eight all-conference players. He also spent six years in the NFL coaching the Oakland Raiders and Indianapolis Colts, where as coach of wide receivers he drafted Reggie Wayne in the first round. As an NFL coach, Norvell coached in six playoff games and coached in Super Bowl XXXVI in 2002 with the Oakland Raiders. He also played one season for the Chicago Bears. He has overseen countless record-breaking moments, including the OU 2010 season, which saw two-time All-American Ryan Broyles, the all-time career receptions leader in college football history, set eight major receiving records and Kenny Stills break the school's receiving records for freshmen.